Mastering
the
Mystical Heptarchy

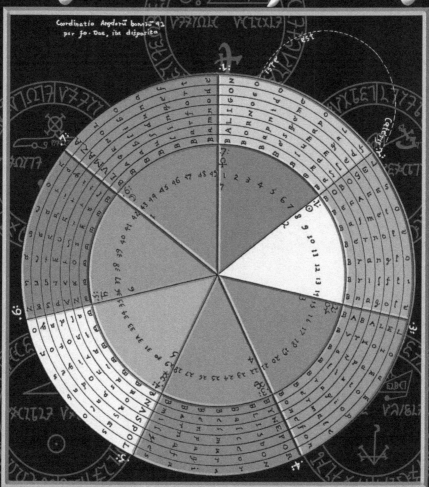

Coordinatio Angelorū bonorū 42
per Jo. Dee, ita disposita

Scott Michael Stenwick

Mastering the Mystical Heptarchy

Scott Michael Stenwick

PENDRAIG Publishing
Los Angeles, CA 91040

Mastering the Mystical Heptarchy
by Scott Michael Stenwick
First Edition © 2011
by PENDRAIG Publishing
All rights reserved.

Edited by   Tony Mierzwicki

Cover Design & Interior Images
Typeset & Layout   Jo-Ann Byers Mierzwicki

PENDRAIG Publishing
Los Angeles, CA 91040
www.PendraigPublishing.com
Printed in the United States of America

ISBN: 978-1-936922-04-8

For Michele Rockne, Odin Brenden,
Keith Strickland, Whitney Holiday, and Maurine Stenwick,
all of whom joined with me in the
heptarchial workings that led to the writing of this book.
May you all accomplish the Great Work
and attain the Summum Bonum,
True Wisdom,
and Perfect Happiness!

Thanks to Joseph H. Peterson
for his wonderful Enochian artwork,
used here with his permission.

Contents

Figures

Tables

Chapter 1
Introduction

The **Heptarchia Mystica**, or *"mystical heptarchy"*, represents a mostly neglected corner of the well-known Enochian magical system revealed to John Dee and Edward Kelley in the late sixteenth century, Dee's only completed grimoire that details the angels attributed to the seven ancient planets. While most modern Enochian magicians are aware of its existence, it is neglected in the sense that very few magicians work with the angels of the heptarchy and for the most part regard them as historical curiosities or some sort of "warm-up" to the later Enochian material that Dee and Kelley received. Because of this I and the members of my magical working group decided to embark on a thorough investigation of this portion of the Enochian magical system starting in 2006. What we found is that the mystical heptarchy represents a powerful and elegant system of ceremonial magick that can be used to accomplish a wide variety of practical objectives.

I draw a distinction between *ceremonial* and *ritual* magick. To most people, and even many practitioners, "ritual magick" and "ceremonial magick" are synonymous, with "ceremonial magick" being the more common term. However, there is an important difference in meaning between the two. In a magical and/or spiritual context, *Ritual* is defined as:

1. an established or prescribed procedure for a religious or other rite.
2. a system or collection of religious or other rites.
3. observance of set forms in public worship.
4. a book of rites or ceremonies.
5. a book containing the offices to be used by priests in administering the sacraments and for visitation of the sick, burial of the dead, etc.
6. a prescribed or established rite, ceremony, proceeding, or service: the ritual of the dead.

Ceremony, on the other hand, is defined somewhat differently in the same context:

2. a formal religious or sacred observance; a solemn rite: a marriage ceremony[1].

Essentially, the difference between the two is that a ritual consists of the necessary instructions for performing a ceremony, whereas a ceremony refers to a specific performance of a given ritual. As I see it, this implies that ceremonial magicians perform pre-existing magical rituals, while ritual magicians write, develop, and test their own magical forms. This distinction is analogous to that found in my own professional field of software development. The ceremonial magician can be thought of as an end-user who runs applications, whereas the ritual magician is akin to a programmer who writes them.

Ceremonial magicians generally work from grimoires, adhering as closely as possible to the ritual as specified in the text. Two recent books[2] have suggested that this ceremonial approach is superior to more eclectic modern ritual methods because the grimoires of the Medieval period that date before about 1350 represent a living tradition of magical practice and in effect represent a "lost art" that can only be restored by

---

1. Definitions from http://www.dictionary.com
2. Ceremonial Magic and the Power of Evocation (Tempe, AZ: Original Falcon Press, 2008) by Joseph Lisiewski and Secrets of the Magical Grimoires (St. Paul, MN: Llewellyn, 2005) by Aaron Leitch

practicing from the original source materials. Whether or not this is true the aspiring ceremonial magician faces with a significant problem — many of these texts are incomplete at best and after being copied from master to student for centuries have accumulated numerous errors. In some cases modern scholars have been able to reconstruct a likely version of the original text, but in other cases this task has simply proved to be too difficult.

What ceremonial magicians really need is a set of lab notes, or if you will, the "source code" for the old grimoires themselves. While we must jump forward two hundred and twenty-some years from the 1350 cutoff in order to find Dee and Kelley's Enochian system, it is quite literally the only example we have of a complex magical system where the original transcripts of the spiritual operations that led to its creation are still available. This leads to a lot of controversy among practitioners and scholars, but the material is also a goldmine for magicians everywhere — the original building blocks of the system are laid out for study in their original context. This system is also by most accounts particularly effective, and in fact enjoys a fearsome reputation among even those magicians who practice the modern form of the system that was modified and elaborated upon by the Hermetic Order of the Golden Dawn and later by Aleister Crowley.

The *"Heptarchia Mystica"* represents the only portion of the Enochian system that was ever assembled into something resembling a workable grimoire. Despite this, many magicians contend that the spirits of the Heptarchia are "inaccessible" or difficult to conjure. I have found that this is true to some extent when working with the *"Heptarchia Mystica"* as written, since Dee assembled it for his own use and included few details regarding his opening and closing procedures which he presumably knew by heart. Furthermore, incorporating certain portions of Dee's later and more widely-used Enochian material seems to enhance the effectiveness of Heptarchial rituals, as do certain ceremonial forms drawn from modern magical practices. These have been included, as the purpose of this book is to present the most effective possible system of Heptarchial magick.

Scott Michael Stenwick
Minneapolis, MN

Chapter 2
A Brief History

Most of the material in this chapter can be found in other books covering the history of Enochian magick in greater detail. As this book is a practical manual, this section is merely an outline of this unique magical system's rich history and background.

John Dee and Edward Kelley

Dr. John Dee, England's most famous Renaissance magician compiled the spirit diaries. They cover a period from 1581 to 1588 and detail his magical operations in which he attempted to enter into communication with the divine. The vast majority of these magical operations were undertaken with the help of Edward Kelley, a scryer who was able to see and hear the spiritual beings conjured by Dee into a shewstone, or crystal. Apparently Dee was one of the first magicians to make use of this technique, and it has permeated our popular culture — even in children's stories, magicians and fortune-tellers use crystal balls to see into the spirit world. Over the course of seven years, various Angels appeared to Dee and Kelly and began teaching them a new system of magick that is today referred to as Enochian, after the biblical patriarch Enoch who "walked with God" following the flood of Noah and was privy to the secrets of the divine world. In his diaries, Dee makes mention of his desire to communicate with God in the same manner in order to obtain the secrets of the natural world, and notes that the shewstone was given to him by the same archangel Uriel who is said to have instructed the Biblical Enoch. At one time a stone believed to be the original shewstone was kept with the Dee collection at the British museum, but it was recently stolen and has not been seen since.

Some sources have described Kelley in a rather unfavorable light, painting him as a charlatan who essentially conned the pious and gullible Dee into believing that he could communicate with spirits. As far as I can tell, the argument that Kelley made the whole thing up is not very tenable. The system appears to be far too comprehensive and consistent for such a thing to be possible without some sort of "mystery grimoire" from which he could have read back memorized sections over time. Various modern occultists have advanced or advocated this theory from time to time, but it can be easily debunked by the fact that no such grimoire or anything similar to it has ever been found to exist. Despite incorporating some elements that appear to have been common to several Renaissance grimoires, the Enochian system is original enough in its structure and use of symbols that it appears to be a unique creation. It is clear that Kelley was instrumental in some way to the creation of the system — from looking at the fragments that have survived of Dee's work with Barnabus Saul, the scryer who worked with Dee prior to Kelley, it is clear that it was not until Kelley's arrival that Dee's magical operations produced anything especially profound. Furthermore, after Kelley's departure in 1588, no records of any significant magical operations performed by Dee have surfaced, although Dee did continue his diaries working with other scryers and a few later fragments of fairly pointless spirit communications survive.

From the historical record, it is clear that both Dee and Kelley share the credit for the success of the magical operations that produced the Enochian system, and as far as I can tell, most modern skeptics are unable to come up with anything more plausible than the story as explained in the spirit diaries themselves — that Dee conjured the spirits into the crystal and Kelley communicated with them as they taught the Enochian system of magick. It is a real testament to the genius of the system that it has survived to this day in myriad forms taught by various magical orders and organizations.

Meric Causaubon

The first publication of any portion of the spirit diaries was *"A True and Faithful Relation of What Passed of Many Years Between Dr. John Dee and Some Spirits"*, edited by Meric Causaubon, in 1659. Causaubon was not an occultist and had no interest in preserving Dee and Kelly's work. He published this portion of the diaries to show that "minions of the Devil" could mislead even a man as intelligent and pious as John Dee. Clearly by this reasoning, the average uneducated person ought not attempt direct communion with the divine and instead seek wisdom from the church. At the same time, however, Causaubon indulged in a bit of tabloid-style promotion of his book, cautioning readers that the volume could be considered "a work of darkness," which of course aroused the curiosity of the public. Regardless of Causaubon's motives, he did play an important role in preserving the spirit diaries for modern occultists, and would perhaps be scandalized that this has become his only real contribution to history.

Elias Ashmole:

Another figure who played a prominent role in the survival of the original documents that comprise the spirit diaries is Elias Ashmole. Ashmole was a contemporary and friend of Meric Causaubon's, but unlike Cauasubon he was a noted esotericist and likely a magician of some sort. I suspect that he encouraged Causaubon to publish the spirit diaries, not to debunk Dee's work but to preserve the diaries for posterity. Ashmole obtained the original copy of the diaries in an unusual manner, which is described in his preface to Dee's *"Mysteriorum Liber Primus"*. Briefly, the documents had been hidden in a secret drawer in a cedar chest that had belonged to Dee. The chest was sold to a Mr. Jones, who eventually discovered the drawer after hearing something rattling around inside the chest. According to the account, approximately half of the papers were lost "under Pyes and other like uses," though it is important to note that few gaps of any significant size can be found in the portion of the diaries relating to

Dee and Kelly's operations. The papers were taken out of the house during the great fire of London, which the chest itself did not survive. Following Mr. Jones' death, his wife went on to marry Thomas Wale, a friend of Ashmole's. Wale traded the diaries to Ashmole in exchange for a copy of a book entitled *"The Institution, Lawes & Ceremonies of the Most Noble Order of the Garter"* in 1672. Ashmole preserved the originals and also made additional copies of the diaries, all of which currently reside in the British Museum.

"Dr. Rudd" and the *Treatise on Angel Magic*:

This late seventeenth-century book was supposedly written by a "Dr. Rudd," though most scholars credit it to one Peter Smart, who was an occultist of the period and most likely used Rudd as a pen name. It is significant to the Enochian system only because of the influence it has had on later occultists including the members of the Hermetic Order of the Golden Dawn. It is a synthetic work that brings together various schools of magic and attempts to cross-reference them to each other, usually in a fairly obvious manner along planetary and elemental lines. The book takes many liberties with the Enochian material, such as attributing the signs of Geomancy to the sixteen sub-quadrants of the Watchtowers along elemental lines, and attributing Goetic demons to the seven Ensigns of Creation along planetary and zodiacal lines. This is an interesting book from a historical standpoint, in that it clearly demonstrates the eclectic nature of the various schools of Angelic magic at the time of its publication, but its Enochian scholarship is highly questionable.

The Hermetic Order of the Golden Dawn:

The first known modern magical order to teach a system incorporating Enochian elements was the Hermetic Order of the Golden Dawn, founded by Dr. Wynn Wescott, Dr. William Woodman, and Samuel L. MacGregor Mathers in England in the year 1887. Israel Regardie published the once secret Golden Dawn teachings in 1937, resulting in the Golden Dawn system becoming one of the most popular systems of ritual magick ever practiced. In fact, many magicians immediately associate Enochian magick with the Golden Dawn, and the version of Enochian taught by that order has become a sort of *de facto* standard in the magical community. This is not necessarily a bad thing, except that it is important not to lose sight of the fact that the Golden Dawn system is not Enochian magick as taught by the Angels to Dee and Kelly. It is a modern synthesis of many traditions and systems, only one of which is found in the Enochian material.

Aleister Crowley:

The English magician Aleister Crowley is another figure who is often associated with the Enochian system in modern times. Demonized by the press of his day, Crowley has been represented at various times as an evil sorcerer, a Satanist, and "the wickedest man in the world." The first published biography of Crowley, John Symonds' *"The Great Beast"*, drew heavily from the popular press and as such served to perpetuate many of the bizarre and inaccurate claims made regarding Crowley during his lifetime. To some extent, Crowley seemed to relish media attention and often gave his critics just enough information to ensure they would assume the worst, though his reputation has suffered among the general public and many occultists as a result. Crowley began his magical career as a Golden Dawn initiate and borrowed heavily from the teachings of that order in his own magical work, so the Enochian system he worked with is more a "dialect" of the Golden Dawn system than his own creation. According to his *"Confessions"*, one of Crowley's regrets was that he had never managed to publish a comprehensive and correct version of the work of Dee and Kelly, which implies that he was aware of the shortcomings of the Golden Dawn material that he did publish in *"The Equinox"*.

Crowley's most impressive piece of work on the Enochian system is *"The Vision and the Voice"*, in which he details visions of the thirty Aires, or Aethyrs, regions of the magical universe that span from the material realm to that of divine source. This is a brilliant, visionary work that highlights Crowley's remarkable scrying abilities; at one point he claimed to be the reincarnation of Edward Kelley. In fact, *"The Vision and the Voice"* contains material that is much more true to the original system of Enochian magick than any of the earlier Golden Dawn embellishments, and I think a very good argument can be put forth that Crowley was really in contact with the same entities as were Dee and Kelley. Much of the material in *"The Vision and the Voice"* influenced Crowley's ideas concerning his own religion/philosophy of Thelema, and there are many parallels between modern Thelemic magick and the original Enochian system. While the original system is very Christian in character, as a Thelemite I have nonetheless had much success working with the system along the original lines with a few modifications to the prayers and conjurations.

Neither Crowley nor the Hermetic Order of the Golden Dawn worked extensively with the spirits of the *"Heptarchia Mystica"*, but rather focused on working with the spirits of the Great Table, which map to the four quarters of the universe known as "watchtowers" in modern parlance, and the Aires. Most modern Golden Dawn and Thelemic magicians do the same, which I believe is why the heptarchial Kings and Princes are often ignored or passed over. The objective of this book is to inspire more magicians to work with these particular entities, as they are quite effective at producing practical magical results and inhabit realms that are relatively unexplored compared to those of other Enochian entities. Diligent performance of the rituals found in this book will enable you to join in this ongoing magical research that seeks to uncover and utilize the power of this remarkable grimoire.

Chapter 3
Source Material

There is a fair amount of debate among scholars concerning the actual origins of the Enochian system. The system is original in many ways, but it is far from completely unique. It incorporates many elements that are similar to those found in other grimoires and texts of magick that were available in the sixteenth century. This is especially true of the mystic heptarchy, which shares a number of common features with other planetary grimoires of the time. Certain of these works are mentioned explicitly within the text of the spirit diaries themselves, and those are the works on which I have focused in my search for influences upon the Enochian system. In addition, it is likely that Dee had copies of most of the grimoires that were in print during his lifetime, since his library at Mortlake was one of the finest in Europe and magick was an area of special interest to him.

***Three Books of Occult Philosophy,* by Henry Cornelius Agrippa:**
These three books comprise the defining work on the state of magical philosophy in the early sixteenth century. Many of the

attributions it details are still used by modern magicians today. The most widely available edition of the "Three Books" is edited by Donald Tyson and is available from Llewellyn.

Agrippa's *Fourth Book of Occult Philosophy*:

There is some debate over whether or not the Fourth Book was actually written by Agrippa himself. It was denounced as a fraud shortly after its publication by one of Agrippa's students in 1567, but some debate still continues concerning its authorship. Regardless of its true origin, the Fourth Book expounds a system of magick based on the symbols and ideas contained in the "Three Books", which contain much source material but no formal ritual practices. Llewellyn published an edition of the "Fourth Book", also edited by Donald Tyson, in 2009.

The *Sworn Book of Honorius*:

This book is a fairly conventional grimoire from the Medieval or Renaissance period. It contains a seal that is remarkably similar to John Dee's Sigillum Dei Aemeth — the lineal figures are identical, but the names written on it are different than those written on the Enochian version. In this case, we need not speculate on the nature of this influence. According to the spirit diaries, the angels directed Dee to the seal in this book and explained that it was the form that was to be used in the construction of the Sigillum, and then proceeded to communicate the correct names that were to be written upon it.

The Steganographia, by Trithemius:

Trithemius was a Hermetic magician and philosopher of the early sixteenth century who is believed to have been Agrippa's teacher, so it is likely that he worked with the system that is detailed in Agrippa's "Three Books". He also wrote several books of his own, including the fascinating *"Steganographia"*. This book is, on the surface, a conventional grimoire that resembles many of the others in publication, but it also contains an intricate system of cryptography. There is in effect an entire second book encoded within the text of the grimoire itself.

Apparently Trithemius originated the idea of a secure socket layer long before computer technology existed. His idea was to encrypt a message that he wished to send using the system outlined in the

"Streganographia" and then summon a spirit, give it the encrypted message, and send it to another magician far away who knew the key to the cipher. This individual would then receive the message from the spirit and decrypt it, with the decryption itself serving as a sort of checksum that proved the message was genuine. It was a far cry from today's secure Internet servers, but the basic idea is the same. There is no word on whether or not the technique worked since none of Trithemius' experimental notes have ever been found.

The Almadel:

There is no reference in the spirit diaries to the *"Almadel"*, another of the grimoires that was in print in the early sixteenth century, but there are many similarities between the system detailed in this book and the mystic heptarchy. The system described in the *"Almadel"* uses a "Table of Art," a square table with a large hexagram in the center reminiscent of the Enochian Holy Table, and contains lists of planetary spirits that are called on specific days of the week, just like the Kings and Princes of the *"Heptarchia Mystica"*.

While you can perform perfectly satisfactory Enochian rituals using just the ritual template in this book and the accompanying texts, there are a number of excellent works available on the Enochian system that go into more detail regarding how and why all of the components are assembled the way they are, why the temple is set up the way it is, how the various conjurations were received, and so forth. John Dee and Edward Kelley have interesting stories of their own above and beyond the seven years they spent detailing their angelic communications, and understanding their motivations will give you greater insight into the way that everything fits together. The following are books that I have enjoyed and recommend as part of a thorough course of Enochian studies.

"Enochian Vision Magick" by Lon Milo DuQuette. Published by Red Wheel/Weiser. Lon DuQuette works using the Golden Dawn/Crowley system and covers how to use it later in the book, but his analysis of the Enochian temple furniture and implements is superb. His opening procedure for Enochian rituals also adapts easily to originalist work, and he does a good job explaining some of the changes and additions made to the Enochian system by the Golden Dawn and Aleister Crowley.

"John Dee's Five Books of Mystery", edited by Joseph H. Peterson. Published by Red Wheel/Weiser. This book includes the sections of Dee's spirit diaries that describe the angels of the *"Heptarchia Mystica"* and which detail most of the Enochian temple furniture. Joseph Peterson is an excellent Enochian scholar and this is the best available edition of the source material. Peterson is also the creator of the artwork depicting the Enochian temple implements that is reproduced in this book.

"Enochian Evocation" by Geoffrey James, published by Heptangle. The original Heptangle edition is out of print, but a facsimile of the book was published as *"The Enochian Magick of Dr. John Dee"* by Llewellyn and it is currently available under the original title from Red Wheel/Weiser. All three editions are the same in terms of content, and I'm not sure why Llewellyn decided to change the title when they published their edition.

"The Hieroglypic Monad (Monas Hieroglyphica)" by John Dee. The current edition is published by Kessinger and available in both English and the original Latin. This work is not directly related to the Enochian material, but it gives a good overview of Dee's ideas about symbols and sacred geometry.

These three are currently out of print, but they contain a lot of good material if you can find them.

"A True and Faithful Relation of What Passed for Many Years Between Dr. John Dee and Some Spirits" by Meric Casaubon. Facsimile edition published by Magickal Childe.

"The Heptarchia Mystica of John Dee", edited by Robert Turner. Published by Aquarian Press.

"Elizabethan Magic: The Art and the Magus" by Robert Turner. Published by Element.

While you need not delve into the inner workings or history of the Enochian system in order to get good magical results, in my experience after a few successful workings most magicians generally develop an interest in doing so.

Chapter 4
The Angelic Language

O ne of the defining characteristics of the Enochian system that sets it apart from other magical systems is that it includes a unique language described as the language of the Angels. Dee and Kelly were told that this was the language spoken by humanity prior to Adam and Eve's expulsion from the Garden of Eden. Dee's notes show that this language consists of twenty-one letters, though as is the case with English some letters can have multiple sounds. Notably, the letter called Gon (I) can be pronounced with a long E vowel sound or a consonant Y, and the letter called Van (V) can by pronounced as a U vowel or consonant V. The letter called Ceph (Z) is sometimes, though not always, pronounced as the syllable "zod," and sometimes as the consonant Z. Otherwise, Dee's pronunciation notes show that most of the words are pronounced as though written in English. This is true of all the spirit names found in the *"Heptarchia Mystica"* as well as the language found in the recitations known as the Angelic Keys or Calls, which will be discussed in Chapter 9.

A quick glance through the Angelic text of the Keys reveals that the words are occasionally difficult to pronounce aloud because as many as three or four consonants are strung together in places. The Golden Dawn solution to this "problem" was to insert extra vowel sounds between the consonants. Using this system, the beginning of the First Key, which is written "OL SONF VORSG GOHO IAD BALT," would be pronounced "ola sonuf vaoresagi goho iada balata" instead of according to Dee's notes, which show that the line is pronounced pretty much as written. I personally prefer the original pronunciation to the longer and more elaborate Golden Dawn pronunciation, and in this case I am a great believer in remaining true to the historical record even when working with Golden Dawn-style Enochian. I do occasionally insert Golden Dawn vowel sounds when pronouncing Angelic words and names, but only between consonant groups that produce a clear glottal stop.

Furthermore, I have found that the more you speak Angelic the easier it becomes to pronounce the words as written. For example, take the word VORSG from the example in the previous paragraph. SG is a sound that does not commonly occur in English, and it seems even more tongue-twisting with the R added to it. One tends to naturally say it as "VORSAG" or "VORSUG," adding an additional syllable between the S and G in much the same way as the Golden Dawn system recommends. However, try saying VORSK. This seems much easier to pronounce because RSK does exist in English and we native speakers are more familiar with it. To say VORSG as written, just replace the K sound with a hard G sound and practice a bit. You will find that while RSG is less familiar it is actually no more difficult to pronounce than RSK. Most of the apparently difficult sounds in the Angelic language can be sounded out in similar ways. In addition, regardless of what the "correct" pronunciation might or might not be, Lon Milo DuQuette makes the good point that as long as you are making a real attempt to speak the language of the angels they should take an interest in you and respond. He uses the analogy that if a mouse were to hop up on a chair and start speaking English you would pay attention, even if it spoke with a thick accent that was hard to understand[1].

Aaron Leitch, author of *"Secrets of the Magical Grimoires"*, has recently come out with his own set of pronunciation notes for the

---

1. Lon Milo DuQuette, Enochian Vision Magick (San Francisco, CA: Red Wheel/Weiser, 2008), 198.

Angelic language, and while for the most part his interpretation of Dee's pronunciation notes is reasonably good there are a couple of glaring problems with it. First of all, there is very little evidence supporting his contention that Angelic letters are ever pronounced by just saying the name of the English letter. I first came across this idea in Leo Vinci's now out of print Enochian dictionary *"Gmicalzoma"* and concluded that it made little sense even back then. For example, in the First Key Leitch contends that DS should be pronounced "dee-es" rather than the more natural "des" or "das" and that CA should be pronounced "see-ay" rather than the obvious "kah." He also contends that NAZPSAD be pronounced "nays-pee-sad" rather than the obvious "nahz-psad" on the grounds that P and S don't combine, so you should just say "pee" for the middle syllable of the word. PS actually combines fine phonetically and is not hard to pronounce; as with SG in the VORSG example, English speakers just are not used to it because it is not a common sound in our language. Try it a few times and you will see what I mean.

While I will say that Leitch should be commended for working off Dee's pronunciation notes rather than the Golden Dawn pronunciation, there are a number of other examples in his lexicon that are questionable at best. He contends that VORSG be pronounced "vorzh" even though the final G is clearly present in Dee's pronunciation notes, that POAMAL should be pronounced "poh-mal" rather than "poh-ah-mal" even though both the O and A appear in Dee's pronunciation notes, and that CICLE should be pronounced "sii-kayl" rather than "kee-kleh" based on the usage of LE in several other unrelated Angelic words. This last idea starts to drift into the same territory as Geoffrey James' attempts in *"Enochian Evocation"* to "correct" the Angelic Keys by resolving what he saw as inconsistencies in the language, when we as non-native Angelic speakers do not necessarily know which sounds should be consistent with each other. Imagine if somebody decided to go through the English language and correct the inconsistencies between different pronunciation of "ough" — through, enough, bough, thorough, and so forth. Who is to say that Angelic is any more regular?

While Dee's notes are sufficiently ambiguous that some of Leitch's pronunciations could very well be more correct than mine, his claims that his version is the first in history to follow the proper principles and that all other scholars working on the pronunciation of the Angelic Keys have "passed over Dee's phonetic notations in silence"[2] should not be taken at face value, especially the latter statement. Geoffrey James published the pronunciation notes themselves in *"Enochian Evocation"* as far back as 1983, Lon Milo DuQuette referred to them in *"Angels, Demons, and Gods of the New Millenium"* in 1997 and of course in his latest book on the subject, 2008's *"Enochian Vision Magick"*, and even David Griffin, head of one of the Golden Dawn lineages, referred to them in *"The Ritual Magic Manual"* published in 1999. In fact, in the late 1990's there was something of a movement among Enochian authors to implement Dee's pronunciation notes in place of the system used by the Golden Dawn, and it surprises me that any Enochian scholar could remain unaware of these publications while studying the system in any detail. Furthermore, just about every online article about Angelic pronunciation at least touches on Dee's notes, and this has been the case for many years.

This table shows the twenty-one Angelic letters along with their names, English equivalents, and sounds.

While most of the tables of letters that are drawn in the spirit diaries are shown with English letters, I use the Angelic characters shown on Table 3 whenever possible for building actual temple

Angelic	Name	English	Sound	Angelic	Name	English	Sound
Ꝟ	Un	A	Short A	Ꝝ	Drux	N	N
Ꝟ	Pa	B	B	ꝲ	Med	O	Long O
Ᏼ	Veh	C	K	Ω	Mals	P	P
Ꝺ	Gal	D	D	Ꝥ	Ger	Q	Q (KW)
Ꝛ	Graph	E	Short E	Ꝼ	Don	R	R
Ꝁ	Or	F	F	Ꝩ	Fam	S	S
Ꝋ	Ged	G	Hard G	Ꝯ	Gisg	T	T
Ꝏ	Na	H	H	Ꝥ	Van	U/V	Short U/V
Ꝉ	Gon	I/Y	Long E/Y	Ᏻ	Pal	X	X
Ꝝ	Ur	L	L	Ꝓ	Ceph	Z	Z/Zod
Ꝫ	Tal	M	M				

Table 1. Angelic Letter Names and Sounds

2. Aaron Leitch, A Pronunciation Guide to the Angelical Language of John Dee (Retrieved 2/3/2009 from http://kheph777.tripod.com/art_angelical_pronunciation.pdf), 2. Leitch has also published a two-volume set entitled The Angelical Language (St. Paul, MN: Llewellyn, 2008) which includes this information.

implements. The Angelic characters are sigils of a sort in their own right that embody the energy of each letter. In this sense, each name can be viewed as a collection of forces. Treating these names as collections of sigils is also useful in the making of talismans, which is discussed in more detail in the chapter on ritual techniques. One of the oddities of the Angelic alphabet is that the name of each letter does not necessarily bear any relation to its sound. This is relevant to the use of letters as sigils since I have found in my own ritual work that these sounds can be used as mantras to call upon the pure force of each letter. However, the individual characteristics of these forces have proved elusive to classify in any concrete or systematic manner. Such attributions are not described in any way in the Spirit Diaries themselves.

There have been many systems of attributions proposed for the Angelic alphabet. The earliest such system that I am aware of is found in Rudd's aforementioned *"Treatise on Angel Magic"*. The system Rudd proposed attributed sixteen of the Angelic letters to the signs of geomancy, and this formed the basis of the later Golden Dawn system of Enochian gematria, or numerology. I have also seen several attempts to relate the Angelic alphabet to the Hebrew alphabet, though this immediately brings up the problem that there is an extra Hebrew letter that must be accounted for. From the standpoint of Qabalistic magick, it would be very desirable to do this because once any alphabet can be mapped to its Hebrew equivalent it can be linked into centuries of Hermetic attributions including the Tree of Life and the Tarot.

I was originally excited by Geoffrey James' publication of one of Dee's versions of the handwritten Angelic alphabet that showed 22 letters, like Hebrew, with the consonant Y as the 22nd letter instead of an alternate pronunciation of the vowel I.[3] However, this does not correspond to the version of the alphabet communicated to Dee and Kelly during their actual operations. It appears to be either a mistake or an attempt by Dee himself to syncretize the Angelic alphabet with Hebrew. The following table shows the Qabalistic attributions determined by the Golden Dawn with Crowley's later additions drawn from *"The Vision and the Voice"*. This system leaves many of the paths empty and doubles up several of the letters, which presents problems for magicians trying to work with the Enochian attributions of the Tree of Life.

3. Geoffrey James, Enochian Evocation (Berkeley Heights, NJ: Heptangle, 1984), 190.

Hebrew	Angelic	English	Value	Hebrew	Angelic	English	Value
Aleph	⟨glyph⟩	H	1	Lamed	⟨glyph⟩	O	30
Beth			2	Mem	⟨glyph⟩	Q	40
Gimel			3	Nun	⟨glyph⟩	N	50
Daleth			4	Samekh	⟨glyph⟩	I	60
Heh	⟨glyph⟩	M	5	Ayin	⟨glyph⟩	V	70
Vav	⟨glyph⟩	A	6	Pe			80
Zain	⟨glyph⟩	S	7	Tzaddi	⟨glyph⟩	B	90
Cheth	⟨glyph⟩	G/L	8	Qoph	⟨glyph⟩	R	100
Teth	⟨glyph⟩	P/Z	9	Resh			200
Yod	⟨glyph⟩	E	10	Shin	⟨glyph⟩	C/D	300
Kaph			20	Tau	⟨glyph⟩	X	400

Table 2 Angelic Gematric Equivalents

Even with only 21 letters available, I have come to the conclusion that there is a reasonable solution to this problem — connect the Hebrew and Enochian alphabets on the basis of pronunciation. Aleister

Hebrew	Sound	Angelic	English	Value
Aleph	A	⟨glyph⟩	A	1
Beth	B	⟨glyph⟩	B	2
Gimel	G	⟨glyph⟩	G	3
Daleth	D	⟨glyph⟩	D	4
Heh	H	⟨glyph⟩	E/H	5
Vav	V	⟨glyph⟩	F/U/V	6
Zain	Z	⟨glyph⟩	Z	7
Cheth	Ch	⟨glyph⟩	X	8
Teth	Soft T	⟨glyph⟩	T	9
Yod	Y	⟨glyph⟩	I/Y	10
Kaph	K	⟨glyph⟩	K	20
Lamed	L	⟨glyph⟩	L	30
Mem	M	⟨glyph⟩	M	40
Nun	N	⟨glyph⟩	N	50
Samekh	S	⟨glyph⟩	S	60
Ayin	O	⟨glyph⟩	O	70
Pe	P	⟨glyph⟩	P	80
Tzaddi	Tz	⟨glyph⟩	Zod	90
Qoph	Q	⟨glyph⟩	Q	100
Resh0	R	⟨glyph⟩	R	200
Shin	Sh	⟨glyph⟩	S	300
Tau	Hard T	⟨glyph⟩	T	400

Table 3 Angelic Alphabet with Attributions

Crowley often used this technique to convert English words into their Hebrew equivalents, and the same will work for the Angelic alphabet. Dee and Kelly were told that Angelic language was in some sense the precursor to Hebrew, so doing this is not much of a deviation from the original revelation. It is not a direct one-to-one correspondence, but it is relatively straightforward. Note that the "English" given for the Hebrew is approximate and simplified, and does not really do justice to the complexity of the Hebrew language in which many of these letters have multiple correct pronunciations depending upon their usage.

While musing on the attributions of the letters is a bit of a departure from the practical mission of this book, working with Enochian gematria of whatever sort is a good way to become more familiar with the letters and the possible relationships between them. One good way to test a spirit that you have summoned is to ask for a word or number, and then later go back to a reference like Crowley's *"Sephir Sephiroth"*[4] or a more recent work like *"Godwin's Cabalistic Encyclopedia"*[5] and see if the number or the valuation of the word corresponds with ideas related to the spirit's supposed nature.

4. Included in Aleister Crowley, 777 and Other Qabalistic Writings (York Beach, ME: Samuel Weiser, 1986).
5. David Godwin, Godwin's Cabalistic Encyclopedia (St. Paul, MN: Llewellyn, 2002).

Chapter 5
The Enochian Temple

Heptarchial operations are performed using a complex set of temple implements that are detailed in John Dee's *"Five Books of Mystery"*. Many modern magicians contend that Enochian magical operations can be worked without any special implements at all, and I will admit that I did so on occasion when I was first exploring the system and some of those workings were indeed successful. However, as I find my magical results significantly improved by the addition of the various temple pieces I highly recommend their use. Furthermore, I have found that much of the "scary" reputation that the Enochian system has acquired over the years seems to be related to people working it without any of the equipment. The next time someone tells you a horror story about a friend or acquaintance who had terrible things happen to them after an Enochian ritual, ask if the person in question even wore an Enochian ring, let alone used the full temple setup. If the story is true, the answer will likely be no.

The angels of the Enochian system are generally accommodating in nature and thus they will tend to adapt themselves to the temple arrangement into which they are summoned. Because of this, your collection of equipment need not be absolutely complete or perfect in order to work with the system, but I have found that the more you have, the better your results become. It is better to have more pieces even if you have to compromise a bit on materials — the ring, for example, is supposed to be made from gold and that is quite an expensive proposition. While a gold ring will certainly produce the best results, I have found that substitute materials such as brass still work reasonably well as long as they have some sort of solar affinity.

The Enochian Ring:

For the proper working of Enochian magick, the Magician must wear a ring inscribed with a specific arrangement of shapes and letters as shown below. The Angels told Dee and Kelly that this was the ring used

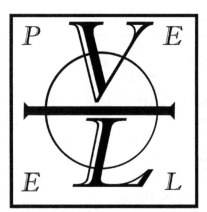

by Solomon to work miracles, although this seems historically unlikely since the letters appear to be those of the English alphabet. I have used a ring with the English characters for many years with good results, and this is the form that most Enochian magicians who wear rings use, but it may be that the letters are supposed to be transcribed into Angelic to obtain the "true" ring.

Figure 1. Face of the Enochian Ring

The notes on the session in which the design of the ring was obtained are not very helpful; they simply include an illustration by Dee showing the design with Latin characters, whereas the Lamen, shown later in the text, includes diagrams in both the Latin and Angelic alphabets.

The letters on the four corners, taken clockwise from the upper left, form the name PELE, which is mentioned in a book that we know Dee worked with because he refers to it in the spirit diaries themselves — Henry Cornelius Agrippa's *"Three Books of Occult Philosophy:"*

> ...and in the book of Judges, the Lord saith, my name
> which is Pele which signifieth with us, a worker of
> miracles, or causing wonders.[1]

The ring is supposed to be made from pure gold, but for financial reasons I have used rings made from other less expensive metals over the years. My first ring was made of silver and suffered an odd fate. After about a year of doing Enochian rituals every week or so, a portion of the band seemed to actually physically disintegrate to the point where a metal-smith friend of mine pronounced it too badly damaged to be worth repairing. According to him, there were micro-fractures all around the band and the ring looked as though it had been pounded on repeatedly with a hammer. As a result, I do not recommend silver for the ring, unless the band is very thick and strong. A friend of mine also has a silver ring with a much thicker band, but oddly enough at some point over the last few years it broke in the same place despite lasting quite a bit longer than mine.

My next ring had a thicker band and was made from a brass. This ring lasted much longer than the silver one and is still intact. Both of those rings seemed to work fine with the Enochian system, so my conclusion is that gold is not an absolute requirement. However, according to the original sources, the use of a ring is absolutely required. The Angels told Dee and Kelly when describing the ring, "Without this, thou shalt do nothing."[2] I have read several books on the system which have understated the importance of the ring, and one which discusses using an "astral ring," which is among the silliest things I have ever heard on this topic. To work the system you will want to use an actual physical ring. Since it does not absolutely need to be of gold, the expense need not be a prohibitive one — make it out of shiny gold cardboard from a craft store if you must, but be sure to wear it. The ring must be worn when doing any sort of Enochian ritual, and in fact I wear mine most of the time.

The addition of the V and L to the letters of PELE may be related to some of Aleister Crowley's Thelemic writings, in that the letters P, V, E, E, L, and L, when transliterated into Hebrew gematria, sum to 156

---

1. Donald Tyson, ed. Agrippa's Three Books of Occult Philosophy (St. Paul, MN: Llewellyn, 1997), 477.
2. Joseph Peterson, ed. John Dee's Five Books of Mystery (York Beach, ME: Red Wheel/Weiser, 2003), 79.

(Pe = 80, Vav = 6, Heh = 5, Heh = 5, Lamed = 30 and Lamed = 30). 156 is also the numeration of the goddess Babalon (Beth = 2, Aleph = 1, Beth = 2, Aleph = 1, Lamed = 30, Ayin = 70, and Nun = 50), who Crowley attributes to Binah, the sphere of Saturn, on the Tree of Life. BABALON is also a word in the Angelic language meaning "to the wicked," which may allude to Saturn's role as a malefic influence in astrology. This relationship also shows up in the *"Heptarchia Mystica"*, in which BNAPSEN, the King attributed to Saturn, explains that through his power the magician may cast out the power of all wicked spirits and may know the doings and practices of evil men.

PELE is actually spelled Peh Lamed Aleph in Hebrew, for a total of 111, which gives different symbolism than the value of the four-letter form. The four-letter form, though, makes the name more similar in structure to the Tetragrammaton, YHVH, and changes the gematria of the transliterated name to 120, which has some interesting numerical properties of its own. 120 can be broken down as 2 * 6 * 10. 2 corresponds to Chockmah, the sphere of the Zodiac; 6 is Tiphareth, the sphere of the Sun; and 10 is Malkuth, the sphere of the elements. Since the Sun is often used to represent planetary energies as a whole, the number 120 can be viewed as a union of elemental, planetary, and zodiac forces, the basic building blocks of the western magical tradition and of the Enochian system.

The circle with a single horizontal line running across it is surprisingly not a symbol that appears in any of the medieval grimoires that Dee was known to possess. It is similar to the alchemical symbol for salt, except that in that symbol the line is contained completely within the circle. Visually, it looks similar to a crude representation of the planet Saturn, which may be related to the symbolism of Babalon mentioned above. Perhaps, though, the best explanation of it can be found in Dee's own writing, the *"Monas Hieroglyphica"*:

THEOREM I

It is by the straight line and the circle that the first and most simple example and representation of all things may be demonstrated, whether such things be either non-existent or merely hidden under Nature's veils.[3]

3. John Dee, The Hieroglyphic Monad (York Beach, ME: Red Wheel/Weiser, 2000), 9.

Since gold is the metal associated with the sun, I think a case can be made that the ring represents a combination of the energies of the Sun and those of Saturn. There is a reference to a ring attributed to the Sun or Saturn in Agrippa's *"Fourth Book of Occult Philosophy"*, which was published only a few years before Dee began his scrying experiments:

> But he that is willing always and readily to receive the oracles of a dream, let him make unto himself a ring of the sun or of Saturn for this purpose.[4]

Dee's goal from the beginning was communication with the Angels, which "the Oracles of a Dream" would clearly accomplish, and this appears to have been his primary motive in practicing magick. Perhaps Dee, Kelley, or the Angels themselves decided to do the *"Fourth Book"* one better and create a ring that combined the energies of these two planetary intelligences.

I recently re-read the original communications regarding the ring and noticed something interesting that may undermine the possible BABALON association, but which opens up another possible set of attributions. The angels did not tell Dee to put a letter V and a letter L on the circle, but "a thing like a V with an L below."[5] They added that the ring had four letters on it, PELE. So perhaps the V and L are not letters but shapes. The V could represent an angle of 60 degrees while the L could represent an angle of 90 degrees. A 60 degree angle is the angle of a triangle when extended into a figure, and the angle of 90 degrees is the angle of a square when extended in the same manner. One of the oddities on the Qabalistic Tree of Life is that there is no path connecting the sphere of Saturn, Binah, with that of Jupiter, Chesed, resulting in the division between the upper three spheres and the lower seven that is referred to as the Abyss. The number of Binah is 3 and that of Chesed is 4, so linking the angle of a triangle to that of a square could geometrically symbolize the opening of the missing path that might allow the divine light to descend more efficiently and cross the boundary between the potential and actual universes.

---

4. Donald Tyson, ed. The Fourth Book of Occult Philosophy (St. Paul, MN: Llewellyn, 2009), 98.
5. Joseph Peterson, ed. John Dee's Five Books of Mystery (York Beach, ME: Red Wheel/Weiser, 2003), 79.

The Lamen:

Like the ring, the lamen should also be worn when performing Enochian rituals. There are two versions of the lamen; according to the Angels, the first was said to have been given by an "illuding spirit"[6] and is not part of the Enochian system. It is similar in form to some goetic symbols, and in that regard appears to more closely resemble sigils from other medieval grimoires than it does the symbols found in the Enochian material.

The "True" lamen presented to Dee and Kelly later looks much more like an Enochian device. It is made up of a grid of Angelic characters arranged in a particular order.

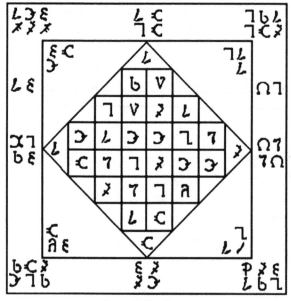

Figure 2. True Lamen

The lamen was supposed to be drawn on parchment, which in those days referred to paper made from animal hide. My original lamen was made from white tagboard, with the Angelic characters on one side and English characters on the other. I went on to construct the lamen I currently use later, which is a brass plate with the Angelic characters engraved on one side. Both are worn around the neck on a cord or chain such that they hang over the chest, covering the anahata chakra or heart center.

---

6. Joseph Peterson, ed. John Dee's Five Books of Mystery (York Beach, ME: Red Wheel/Weiser, 2003), 68.

The Robe:

According to the spirit diaries, the robe worn when working with the Enochian system should be white, unadorned, and, if possible, made from linen. I use a simple white linen tau-shaped robe, which conforms exactly to the text, but was expensive to make and is rather scratchy. I have also used robes made from other natural fibers such as cotton, which are easy to procure and less expensive, with good results. The plain white robe is described in several of the medieval grimoires and represents purity and holiness, which is why it is simple and unadorned.

The Holy Table:

The Holy Table is the centerpiece of an Enochian temple. The Angels specified that it should be approximately three feet square with legs of the same height, and made from "sweet wood." One writer, Geoffrey James, has suggested cedar,[7] which was sometimes referred to as "sweet" during the period in question. On the top of the Table is painted a set of lineal figures and Angelic characters in yellow. A likely influence on this design can be found in the *"Almadel"*, which makes use of a square table with a large hexagram in the center, although the design uses Hebrew characters and also incorporates four pentagrams at the corners.

The Holy Table represents Tiphareth, the sphere of the Sun on the Tree of Life, as can be easily ascertained from Hermetic Qabalistic attributions. Yellow is the color of Tiphareth, and the hexagram, which is prominently displayed in the center of the table, is its lineal figure. These attributions are still in use among ritual magicians today and can be found in Agrippa's *"Three Books of Occult Philosophy"*. Also, the Table occupies the center of an Enochian temple, and Tiphareth is the central sphere on the Tree of Life.

One of the difficulties in constructing a working table is that some of the figures in Meric Causaubon's *"True and Faithful Relation"* are inverted right to left. While the letters of the table itself are switched, other diagrams that appear in the same image are not inverted or reversed. This suggests that the reversal was either a deliberate blind on the part of Causaubon to keep magicians from using the system effectively or a serious error on the part of the printer. For whatever

---

7. Geoffrey James, Enochian Evocation (Berkeley Heights, NJ: Heptangle, 1984), 181.

reason, it is easy enough to look through the diagrams and then read the communications describing them and see that the diagram of the table is a mirror image of the description given. The correct design is shown below.

A good inexpensive way to build a Holy Table is to pick up a 3 foot square card table. They are still often built to the exact dimensions recommended to Dee and Kelley, 3 feet square with four 3-foot legs. Finding one with a wooden surface is ideal, but if that proves too difficult or costly you can go ahead and draw the appropriate figures onto the top with acrylic paint or even permanent marker. This won't work quite as effectively as a Table corresponding to the original specifications, but it should be sufficient.

Figure 3. Holy Table

Not being a great woodworker, my Holy Table is just a tabletop. It is a three-foot square piece of high-grade red oak plywood, trimmed with decorative molding and finished with mahogany-tinted tung oil. I used bright yellow acrylic paint for the diagrams and characters, which produces a nice luminous effect by candlelight in contrast to the darker wood. My attempts to add legs that could be easily removed failed miserably and resulted in a Table that could barely stand, so I finally gave up and found a table of about the right size to serve as a base for the tabletop. Removable legs are useful should you ever want to put a very heavy object, or even a person, onto the Table for some specific ritual purpose, because once they are removed the tabletop can be placed directly on the floor of the temple.

The Sigillum Dei Aemeth:

Figure 4. Top of the Sigillum Dei Aemeth.
The image is large to show the detail and on its own page to facilitate photocopying. The asterisk below the Y/14 square near the bottom of the diagram indicates that some experts believe the number in the square should be 15 rather than 14.

The Sigillum Dei Aemeth (*"True Seal of God"*) is a pantacle, or disk, that is placed in the center of the Holy Table. It should be nine inches in diameter and made from pure wax, though paraffin may be an acceptable modern substitute. The top bears the design at left *(fig. 4)*, which may be easier to cast in some fashion than manually engrave into the wax due to its complexity.

The bottom, on the other hand, bears the design shown below, which is much simpler and not at all difficult to engrave by hand. Mine was originally cast without it, so I manually cut the design into the back of my Sigillum as part of the consecration ritual. I have yet to see a Sigillum for sale anywhere that has a properly engraved bottom, so if you buy one somewhere be aware that you will probably have to cut or engrave the design on the back side yourself.

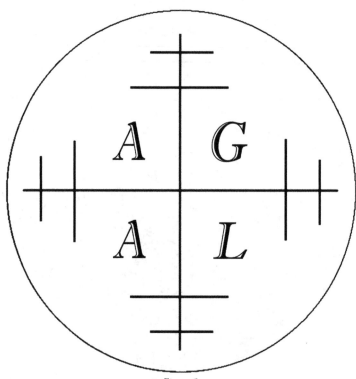

Figure 5.
Bottom of Sigullum Dei Aemeth.
It is sized to match the previous diagram, again for photocopying purposes.

Exotic materials aside, one way to construct your own Sigillum right now is to photocopy both sides out of this book and paste them together or onto something like a wooden or cardboard disk. The result is not as impressive as a full-sized wax pantacle, but it should prove serviceable. You could also melt down some wax in a cake pan or kettle of the right size to form it into a disk and then glue the photocopied top and bottom onto it.

Colin Campbell has recently published a book entitled *"The Magic Seal of Dr. John Dee"* in which he puts forth the idea that Dee made several errors in constructing what has become the standard representation of the Sigillum.[8] I attended a lecture by Campbell in 2009 in which he explained what those errors were and how they could be rectified in order to make the device more effective than it already is. While I usually find that new hypotheses about the Enochian system are full of speculation, especially when they contradict the original Dee material, I was very impressed with Campbell's research and his rationale for concluding that a more correct version of the Sigillum could indeed be constructed. As a result I highly recommend that you pick up and read through Campbell's book, especially if you are planning on carving your own wax Sigillum rather than copying the one shown here.

Dee noted regarding the Sigillum Dei Aemeth that "Oute of this Circle shall no creature pass."[9] What I have found in ritual is that the Table amplifies and collects magical energy and the Sigillum contains it. The basic form of the Sigillum is that of a pentagram, symbolizing the elemental or microcosmic world, surrounded by a heptagram, symbolizing the action of the seven ancient planets and the macrocosmic world. Various Angelic names can be extracted from the outer ring, though the names of these Angels do not appear to figure prominently in the Enochian Conjurations or Invocations. These names, their complex method of extraction, and their deep and multifaceted symbolism are fully explained in Lon Milo DuQuette's *"Enochian Vision Magick"*, and rather than expounding all of them here I instead direct you to DuQuette's work which is the most excellent and complete expostulation of the Sigillum that I have ever come across.[10]

---

8. Colin Campbell, The Magic Seal of Dr. John Dee (York Beach, ME: Teitan Press, 2009).

9. Joseph Peterson, ed. John Dee's Five Books of Mystery (York Beach, ME: Red Wheel/Weiser, 2003), 113.

10. Lon Milo DuQuette, Enochian Vision Magick (San Francisco, CA: Weiser Books, 2008), 55-78.

Figure 6.
Design for the 4 small Sigils, front and back.

In addition to the primary Sigillum that occupies the center of the Holy Table, smaller copies of it, four and a half inches in diameter, should be placed under each of the Tables's four legs. As my Table lacks permanent legs I generally omit this portion of the temple setup, but my suspicion is that if your construction skills are superior to mine you will find that having them adds to the effectiveness of the temple setup.

Smaller images of the top and bottom are shown here, again for photocopying purposes. They can be constructed in the same manner as the larger version.

The Ensigns of Creation:

Figure 7. Holy Table with Positions of Sigillum Dei Aemeth and Ensigns

The Ensigns of Creation are seven talismans that are placed on the Holy Table surrounding the Sigillum Dei Aemeth. They were originally supposed to be made from purified tin, but later Dee and Kelly were told to paint them onto the table itself using blue for the lines and red for the characters and letters. My compromise solution is tagboard; I like being able to have separate talismans that can be removed and used as planetary talismans for rituals that do not require the table, but at the same time tin can be difficult to procure and work with. The seven Ensigns are arranged evenly around the Sigillum Dei Aemeth as shown here.

The attribution of each Ensign can be inferred from the wheel of the mystical heptarchy; considering their number as well as their placement on the Table and their close association with the Heptarchial Angels, it is clear that the Ensigns are planetary in nature. By comparing the position of each planet on the wheel to the location of each Ensign the following attributions can be determined. The images of the Ensigns shown here can be photocopied, just like those of the Sigillum.

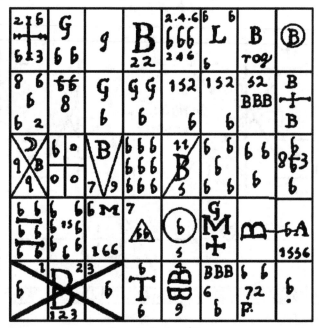

Figure 8. Ensign of Venus

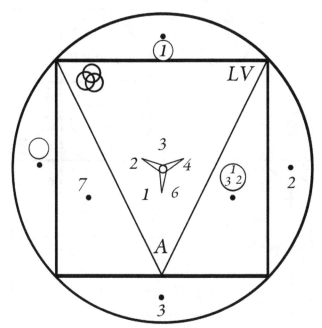

Figure 9. Ensign of the Sun

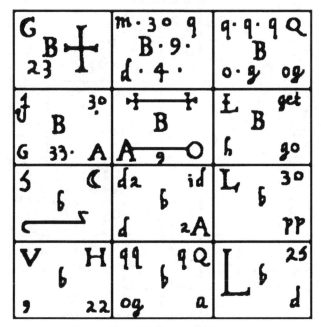

Figure 10. Ensign of Mars

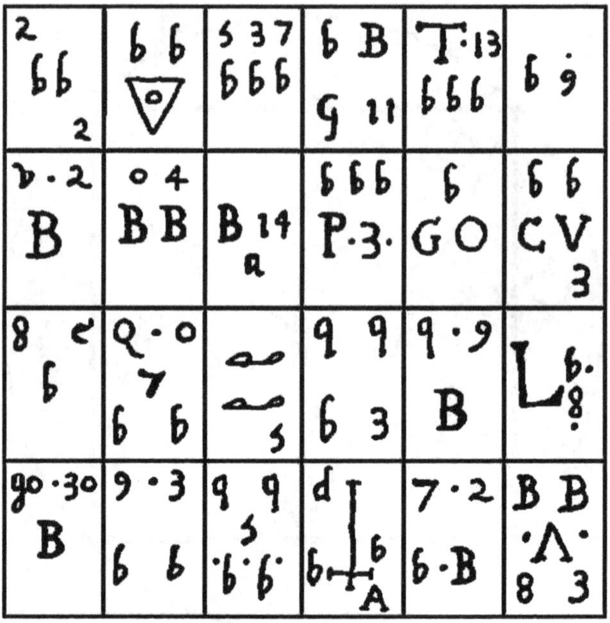

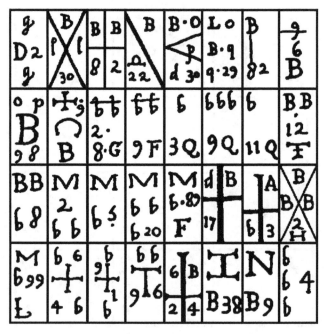

Figure 11. Ensign of Jupiter

Figure 12. Ensign of Mercury

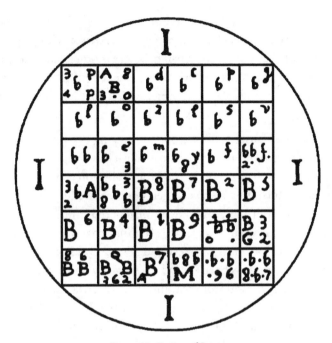

Figure 13. Ensign of Saturn

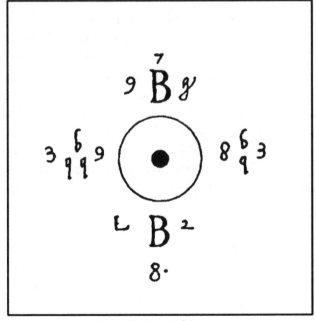

Figure 14. Ensign of the Moon

On my own Holy Table, I sometimes augment the Ensigns by placing a candle of the color of each planet as found in Aleister Crowley's *"Liber 777"* on top of the appropriate Ensign. There is no real justification for this in the Dee and Kelly material itself, but I find it to be useful for keeping in mind which planet occupies which position on the Table.

The Shewstone:

Dee and Kelly used a Shewstone, or scrying crystal much like the fairy-tale "crystal ball," to communicate with the Enochian angels. The stone was placed in the center of the Holy Table, on top of the Sigillum Dei Aemeth, and Kelly, a scryer, then concentrated on the stone and would see visions of the Angels, who instructed him in the workings of the Enochian system. It is in this manner that virtually all of the Enochian source material was received. Dee's obsession with scrying and communication has been picked up by many modern practitioners of Enochian magick, and from reading some accounts one might be led to think that this is all the system is good for. In fact, the Enochian system is also an incredibly powerful system of practical magick and you do not need to be able to scry well in order to cast practical spells that are likely to work.

The center of the Holy Table, directly above the Sigillum Dei Aemeth, is the focal point of any ritual involving the Table. Dee and Kelly were primarily interested in obtaining knowledge of the Enochian system itself via communication with the Angels, so for the most part their rituals used the shewstone as the central focus of all their work. In Enochian sorcery, you will want to use a variety of objects. I use candles fairly often, normally of a color related by Qabalistic attributions to the intended result of the ritual. I have also used crystals, and for healing rituals I often set the table on the floor of the temple and have them sit within the Table itself holding Sigillum. Also, if you are empowering a talisman or other magical implement the object that is to receive the charge should be used as the focus.

In effect, the Sigillum acts much like the triangle used in Goetic operations. It is a microcosm of the universe that the magician can control by summoning spirits such as the heptarchial angels into the area directly above it. In order to cast spells at a distant target you will want to place a magical link such as a photograph onto the Sigillum along with the candle or any other additional focus. The use of magical links in this manner is a basic practical technique, and relies on the two primary laws of sympathetic magick, Contagion and Similarity. A contagion link is created when two objects come into contact, and a similarity link is created between two objects that resemble one another. In a ritual context, then, one may represent the other. For example, let's say that you were casting a healing spell on someone not present in the temple. If you have a photograph of the person you can place it in the center of the Sigillum and then the angel you summon will be able to affect him or her through the link.

The Cloth:

The Sigillum, Ensigns, and Holy Table should be covered with a cloth of either red silk or "changeable red and green silk," presumably some sort of double-weave. Dee recommends both in different places in the diaries and as far as I can tell either will work. Most modern magicians who assemble temples use red cloth and there is some flexibility in terms of material. Silk, which Dee was directed to use, is best but natural fibers of whatever sort such as cotton will also work. Something as simple as a small red blanket could work for this purpose. The design drawn by Dee shows tassels on the corners of the cloth, but keep in mind that the cloth should not be large enough for the cloth or tassels to reach the floor.

The Carpet:

The floor under the Holy Table should likewise be covered with a red carpet also made from silk. It is possible to find oriental-style rugs made from red silk, and though they are expensive they are just about the best solution to the problem. You can also use something like a sheet of red fabric or a red blanket, but make sure that you can walk comfortably around the Holy Table without disturbing the carpet too much or tripping over it. This is a case where it probably is better to work without the carpet than to try and make do with light fabric that could easily distract you in the middle of reading the Keys or Conjurations.

The Book:

Dee was told to make a book containing all of the prayers, invocations, and conjurations that he and Kelley received so that he could read the various texts in ritual. In this, at least, your task is already done, at least for those involving the spirits of the Heptarchia Mystica — you're holding that book in your hands right now. The ritual template in the next chapter contains all of the necessary page references to flip back and forth between the appropriate texts for any sort of operation supported in the system in order to work with the system, but I have found that the more you have, the better your results become. It is better to have more pieces even if you have to compromise a bit on materials — the ring, for example, is supposed to be made from gold and that is quite an expensive proposition. While a gold ring will certainly produce the best results, I have found that substitute materials such as brass still work reasonably well as long as they have some sort of solar affinity.

Chapter 6
Heptarchial Ritual Temple

It is my intention that you as an aspiring magician should be able to pick up this book and begin working magick right away. Some authors are more cautious than I am in this regard, but in my experience much of that fear comes from the thoroughly outdated magical paradigms of previous centuries. Magick was once thought to be dangerous, not just to the practitioner's soul but also to everyone around him or her. It was believed that this was because magick was ruled by demonic forces that looked for any opportunity to get out of hand and wreak havoc. In addition, the power of magick was thought to be related to secrecy, in that hidden knowledge was considered to be more powerful than public knowledge. It was thus believed that the exposure of magical techniques would undermine their efficacy.

Both of these ideas are fundamentally incorrect. The first is rooted in the paranoid worldview of the medieval church that gave rise to the Inquisition and witchcraft trials, and the second has restricted magical development for over a thousand years. Today we finally can see how the rise of the Internet and related communications technology contribute to the growth of magical ideas rather than sapping their strength. Practiced properly, magick is both a science and an art — not a hard science like physics, but maybe a soft one like psychology in its early days. Magicians keep journals of their practices, carefully noting their successes and failures, and whenever possible conduct empirical experiments to test their progress. If enough working magicians were to share their results, the resulting knowledge base would allow for more formal research into the nature of magical powers and might even allow us to duplicate magical effects using some sort of technology.

There is a third class of argument against jumping in and doing magick right away that I find particularly annoying, and that is the person who claims that you are somehow "degrading the art" by using it for practical purposes. These people are generally either profoundly unsuccessful people who treat their poverty like a badge of office, trust fund kids who have never really needed to work at making a living, or simply individuals who want to feel spiritually superior without doing any work. The whole point of this argument is either to justify what on the outside looks like failure, or to keep the person making it from being exposed as an inferior practitioner with delusions of grandeur. The bottom line is that there is nothing virtuous about suffering, and there is nothing wrong with using magical powers to set up your life so that you are richer, happier, and more successful. Even from a purely theurgic point of view a stress-free life contributes positively to the successful pursuit of spiritual illumination. You can spend a bunch of time meditating to lower your stress, or you can set up your Enochian temple and conjure away the root of the problem. Better still, you can do both.

Finally, the most vehement opposition to magical practice usually comes from professional skeptics. I have no problem with people who are genuinely skeptical and based on their own experience have found little use for spiritual practice in their own lives. However, there is a certain species of skeptic who delights in debunking any phenomenon that lies beyond the controlled experimentation of the scientific method, even going so far on occasion as to dishonestly rig the game in their favor. Such people see magick as at best a waste of time, and at worst a hopeless and outdated superstition, leading them to ridiculously insist that astrology columns in newspapers, or television programs about the paranormal will, inevitably lead to the burning of accused witches in modern America. Such skeptics do perform valuable services such as exposing confidence artists masquerading as magicians, but I also find them irrationally closed-minded about any phenomenon that is uncommon or outside what they consider normal experiences. My advice to anyone who is interested in magick but finds skeptical arguments compelling? Try it and see for yourself if it works, and never let a good debater talk you into denying your own experiences.

The angels made it clear to Dee and Kelley that much of the Enochian material was intended to be read from the book, so the entire ritual text does not necessarily need to be memorized by the aspiring Enochian magician. The ritual templates in this chapter incorporate ideas from my own professional field of software development and are technical documents that will allow you to perform Enochian rituals right out of this book. Simply start at the beginning and work your way through, flipping to the appropriate page as instructed. It is useful to get bookmarks of some sort that you can use to mark the template along with the other sections of text that you will be reciting for each ritual that you perform. Having used other less organized books for this purpose, I have found that this technique makes rituals flow much more smoothly than having to scan through page numbers between the various ritual sections.

This template uses the standard Enochian temple setup detailed in Chapter 4, which you should assemble to the best of your ability including as many elements as you can practically incorporate. Wear the Enochian ring, lamen, and white robe. Place the focus of your spell in the center of the Sigillum on top of the cloth so that it is visible. You will begin the ritual standing to the west of the Holy Table facing east, and the Table should be oriented in such a way that with the cloth off you can read the letters on it right side up. When working these rituals you always face the Holy Table when performing the Keys and conjurations, so that when you are casting to the east you should stand to the west of the Table, when casting south you should stand to the north of the Table, and so forth.

Note that the template marks a number of the steps as "optional." These consist of modern ceremonial forms and procedural modifications such as the use of the First and Second Angelic Keys, none of which are drawn from the text of the *"Heptarchia Mystica"*. I have found that in my own work these additions profoundly enhance the effectiveness of the heptarchial system, but at the same time I understand that they may not be appealing to magicians who would rather work with the old grimoires as written. Such magicians should feel free to skip these optional steps.

I. Heptarchia Mystica Ritual Template

0. Preparation

Set up the Enochian temple to the best of your ability as described in Chapter 5. Wear the Enochian ring, robe, and lamen. Stand to the west of the Holy Table facing east.

1A. Opening the Temple — Ceremonial (optional)

A. Perform the banishing AOEVEAE pentagram ritual (page 67). Alternatively, you may open the temple with the Golden Dawn Lesser Banishing Ritual of the Pentagram or Aleister Crowley's Star Ruby.

B. If you intend your ritual to have a macrocosmic effect that extends beyond the psychological realm, perform the invoking MADRIAX hexagram ritual (page 70). Alternatively, if you opened with the LBRP you should perform the Lesser Invoking Ritual of the Hexagram, or if you opened with the Star Ruby you should perform the Star Sapphire. The combination of a banishing pentagram ritual and an invoking hexagram ritual forms an operant field as explained in Chapter 6.

1B. Opening the Temple — Devotional

Perform the Prayer of Enoch (page 76). This prayer may be performed on its own to open the temple, or it may follow the ceremonial opening performed as step 1A.

2. The Preliminary Invocation

A. Perform the NAZ OLPIRT energy work exercise (optional) (page 82).

B. Perform the original or revised Oration to God (page 85).

3. The Opening Keys (optional)

A. For an evocation, intone the First Key in Angelic followed by English. (page 92).

B. For an invocation, intone the Second Key in Angelic followed by English (page 93).

C. For a ritual including both evocatory and invocatory elements, perform the First Key (page 92) followed by the Second Key (page 93). If you are working with another person like Dee and Kelley did, with one person acting as magician and the other as scryer, the magician should read the First Key followed by the scryer reading the Second Key.

4. Tuning the Space

A. Your ritual should be scheduled so that it is being performed on the appropriate day and during the proper planetary hour as explained in Chapter 10.

B. Perform the Greater Ritual of the Hexagram corresponding to the King or Prince that you are evoking as shown in Chapter 10 (optional). Note that the planetary attribution will match that of the day for the Kings, but will be different for the Princes. Also, this ritual should only be performed here if the temple was opened using the ceremonial method.

5. The Conjuration

Place the appropriate talisman for the King or Prince on the floor and stand upon it. Then intone the appropriate conjuration based on the following table.

Day of the Week	King	Conjuration	Prince	Conjuration
(Any)	Carmara	Page 124	Hagonel	Page 133
Sunday	Bobogel	Page 125	Bornogo	Page 134
Monday	Blumaza	Page 126	Bralges	Page 135
Tuesday	Babalel	Page 127	Befafes	Page 136
Wednesday	Bnaspol	Page 128	Blisdon	Page 137
Thursday	Bynepor	Page 129	Butmono	Page 138
Friday	Baligon	Page 130	Bagenol	Page 139
Saturday	Bnapsen	Page 131	Brorges	Page 140

Table 4. The Kings and Princes

6. The Charge to the Spirit

Deliver the Charge to the spirit or spirits that you have personally composed according the instructions given in Chapter 12 (page 143).

7. Closing the Temple

A. Perform the License to Depart (page 152).

B. For rituals opened using the ceremonial method, conclude the MADRIAX (page 70) and AOEVEAE (page 67). Alternatively, if the ritual was opened with the Golden Dawn Lesser Rituals of the Pentagram and Hexagram, perform the Lesser Banishing Ritual of the Pentagram for a ritual that has only an external target or the Qabalistic Cross by itself for a ritual that is intended to affect the magician exclusively or both the magician and an external target. For the Star Ruby/Star Sapphire the same rules apply — close with either the Star Ruby or that ritual's form of the Qabalistic Cross depending upon the ritual's target.

C. Declare the temple closed. The ritual is now complete.

Chapter 7
Opening the Temple

The most basic ceremonial opening forms used by modern magicians are the Lesser Ritual of the Pentagram and Lesser Ritual of the Hexagram that originated with the magicians of the Golden Dawn tradition. The original rituals that I have included in this chapter can be used in a similar manner, and have the added advantage that they are truly Enochian rituals tailored for the Enochian system. I will, however, make a quick mention of a correction to what is usually taught as the proper way to perform these two rituals because this correction informs the design of my Enochian opening rituals. Pentagram and hexagram rituals can be performed as either banishing or invoking rituals. Most teachers will tell you that you should open and close your rituals with the Lesser Banishing Ritual of the Pentagram followed by the Lesser Banishing Ritual of the Hexagram. In fact, this combination of rituals does not work well for most magical operations, and I am unsure whether it represents a deliberate misrepresentation or a corruption of the original Golden Dawn rituals.

I started researching the Golden Dawn ritual forms many years ago and was confused by how little material was available on the invoking versions of these rituals and when they should be used. In Aleister Crowley's *"Liber O vel Manus et Sagittae"* I found it curious that he covered the Lesser Banishing Ritual of the Pentagram followed by an explanation of the Lesser Invoking Ritual of the Hexagram. I went ahead and decided to try this combination despite all of the recommendations against it, and was absolutely blown away by my results — all of a sudden my practical magical work got a whole lot better. I set up a number of objective probability tests and, sure enough, the LBRP/LIRH was amazing. I could not get anywhere near the same level of effectiveness with the LBRP/LBRH. When I discovered this I asked around the magical community and, sure enough, most of the magicians who I knew who were able to get good results using the Golden Dawn forms had figured out the same thing.

So what could be going on here? My best guess is that most modern writers do not understand how to use these two rituals correctly, and this may even be the reason that many traditional grimoire practitioners argue that the Golden Dawn methods do not work, or at least do not work well. The Lesser Ritual of the Pentagram represents the psychological realm or microcosm and the Lesser Ritual of the Hexagram represents the physical realm or macrocosm. Together the rituals set up a space in which the relationship between microcosm and macrocosm is defined. I refer to this space as a *Field*. The four combinations of the banishing and invoking forms of the two rituals set up four different fields that correspond to specific classes of magical operations.

Banishing Field (LBRP/LBRH):

> This is how most magicians begin their rituals when working with the Golden Dawn forms. It is, in effect, the "full shutdown" — it clears mental and spiritual forms from both the interior and exterior worlds. It can be used to completely cleanse a temple, banish spirits permanently, or neutralize a magical effect that is targeting the magician. What it also does, though, is shut down any ongoing spells that the magician has running unless they are bound to talismans or

some anchor other than the magician's personal consciousness. If you are casting a spell that you want to work over the next week, do not end the ritual with this combination under any set of circumstances unless you're convinced you made a mistake and want to stop the spell. The effect that you just set in motion will be negated the minute that the banishing field goes up.

Invoking Field (LIRP/LIRH):

This combination energizes all ongoing magical effects, and can be used to begin a ritual that you want to operate in both the interior and exterior worlds. A good example of this is a spell to get a good job. You want the spell to affect your psyche in such a way that you seem more confident and capable, but you also want it to shift probabilities in the material world so that the right opportunity will come your way.

Centering Field (LIRP/LBRH):

This combination sets up a field in which the interior world is engaged while influences from the exterior world are neutralized. This field is ideal for exclusively psychological magical work of all sorts.

Operant Field (LBRP/LIRH):

This field clears the interior world and then merges it with the exterior world, setting up a space in which thought more easily becomes material reality. All of the energy of a spell cast within this field is targeted on the macrocosm and the resulting probability shifts show that magick done this way just influences the outside world better — significantly better.

Of these four the operant field is the primary field that you should be using when working with Enochian sorcery, and as a result this is the field that is set up when you follow the instructions in the template. You should always banish before you invoke, and thus the centering and invoking fields should be preceded by an initial LBRP. This makes their use somewhat more cumbersome, since the sequence you wind up with is LBRP/LIRP/LIRH and LBRP/LIRB/LBRH.

The Lesser Ritual of the Pentagram:

This ritual can be found in just about any introductory book on ritual magick, particularly those covering the Golden Dawn and Thelemic traditions. While I am including the text of the ritual and some brief notations here for the sake of completeness, if you are a beginning magician you should do some additional research regarding how to do the visualizations, vibrations, breathing, and so forth correctly.[1] It should be committed to memory rather than read out of this book or any other.

1. Stand facing east. With the thumb of your right hand touch your forehead and intone ATEH (ah-TAY). Then trace down the center of your body to your genital area and intone MALKUTH (mal-KOOT), trace back up to the center of your chest then over to your right shoulder and intone VE GEBURAH (VAY geh-boo-RAH), then trace across to your left shoulder and intone VE GEDULAH (VAY geh-doo-LAH). Finally, clasp your hands over the center of your chest and intone LE OLAHM, AMEN (LAY oh-LAHM, ah-MEN). This first section is called the Qabalistic Cross and can be performed on its own as a basic centering exercise. As you trace, visualize a cross of glowing white brilliance forming over your body, representing the Qabalistic Tree of Life.

Figure 15.
Banishing Pentagram of Earth

Figure 16.
Invoking Pentagram of Earth

2. In the east, trace the appropriate Pentagram of Earth and vibrate YHVH (yah-WAY or Yod Heh Vav Heh). The pentagram should be visualized as formed from living fire.

---

1. One of the most popular introductory books of all time on Golden Dawn magick is Donald Michael Kraig's Modern Magick (St. Paul, MN: Llewellyn, 2010), originally published in 1988 and now in its third edition. Kraig is a good writer and covers a lot of material. However, his method of teaching certain rituals such as the Lesser Hexagram differs substantially from mine. He teaches that you should open every ritual with both the LBRP and LBRH – the banishing field – which in my experience substantially limits your magical power. If you decide to study his book and like his reasoning go ahead and see if his method works better for you, but my suspicion is that it will not. In terms of what modern GD orders teach, his method is much more standard than mine, but the experimentation that I've done comparing them is quite extensive and my field method always comes out ahead in terms of practical results.

3. Turn to the south. Trace the appropriate Pentagram of Earth and vibrate ADNI (ah-doh-NYE).

4. Turn to the west. Trace the appropriate Pentagram of Earth and vibrate AHIH (eh-hi-YAY).

5. Turn to the north. Trace the appropriate Pentagram of Earth and vibrate AGLA (ah-guh-LAH).

6. Return to face the east. Extend your arms in the form of a cross and intone:

> Before me RAPHAEL (rah-fay-EL),
> Behind me GABRIEL (gah-bree-EL),
> On my right hand MICHAEL (mee-kye-EL),
> On my left hand URIEL[2] (oo-ree-EL).
> For about me flames the pentagram,
> And in the column stands the six-rayed star.

As you vibrate the name of each Archangel visualize the appropriate figure standing in the corresponding direction. Raphael in the east wears a yellow robe and holds a caduceus wand, Gabriel in the west wears a blue robe and holds a chalice, Michael in the south wears a red robe and holds a flaming sword, and Uriel in the north wears a black robe and holds a scythe.

For the final two lines, you first visualize a pentagram forming over your body and then on the last line visualize yourself standing within a vertical hexagonal pillar of light inscribed with a hexagram. For the pentagram visualization, imagine yourself as Leonardo Da Vinci's Vitruvian Man with an upright pentagram inscribing the circle in the drawing. For the hexagram visualization, imagine your entire body within a round column of light extending from floor to ceiling and beyond. The hexagram then inscribes the cross-section of the pillar at a right angle relative to the vertical plane of the pentagram.

7. Repeat step 1, the Qabalistic Cross.

---

2. Most magical orders teach the final Archangel name as AURIEL rather than URIEL. I like to use the latter name for Enochian operations because John Dee notes URIEL as the fourth Archangel rather than AURIEL.

The Lesser Ritual of the Hexagram:

Like the Lesser Ritual of the Pentagram, this ritual can be found in most introductory books on Golden Dawn and Thelemic magick. As with the Lesser Ritual of the Pentagram you will want to commit it to memory. Also, before using this ritual you will want to do some additional research above and beyond the instructions given here if you are unfamiliar with it. The main pitfall to watch out for is authors who teach that you should open or close rituals using only the banishing form. As I mentioned at the beginning of this chapter, this method will greatly undermine your ability to work effective magick.

1. Stand facing east following the performance of the Lesser Ritual of the Pentagram. Intone the following:

   INRI – Yod Nun Resh Yod.
   Virgo, Isis, mighty mother,
   Scorpio, Apophis, destroyer,
   Sol, Osiris, slain and risen,
   Isis, Apophis, Osiris,
   IAO.

   This section is called the Keyword Analysis.

2. Give the Sign of Osiris Slain, extending both arms in the form of a cross. Say:

   Osiris slain![3]

   Then give the Sign of the Mourning of Isis. With open hands bend both elbows at 90 degree angles, raising the right forearm to point up and dropping the left forearm to point down. The right palm should be up and facing forward and the left should be down and facing backwards. Turn slightly to your left and look down. Say:

   The Mourning of Isis!

   Then give the Sign of Apophis and Typhon, raising both arms straight above your head and holding them apart at an angle of about sixty degrees. The wrists

---

3. The traditional Golden Dawn teaching regarding the first four statements in this section is to add "The Sign of" to the beginning of each. In practice I find this to be choppy and awkward, so when using this ritual I perform it as shown here.

should be straight, the hands open, and the palms toward each other. Say:

Apophis and Typhon!

Then give the Sign of Osiris Risen. Cross your arms on your chest, left over right, like an Egyptian mummy. The hands should be open with your right palm on your left shoulder and your left palm on your right shoulder. Say:

Osiris risen!

Repeat the Sign of Osiris Slain and say:

L – V – X – LUX.

Repeat the Sign of Osiris Risen and say:

The light of the Cross.

This section is called the Signs of LVX.

3. Trace the appropriate Hexagram of Fire in the east as you vibrate ARARITA. The two upward triangles should be visualized in red.

Figure 17.
Invoking Hexagram of Fire

Figure 18
Banishing Hexagram of Fire

4. Turn to the south. Trace the appropriate Hexagram of Earth in the south as you vibrate ARARITA. The upward triangle should be visualized in red and the downward triangle should be visualized in blue.

Figure 19.
Invoking Hexagram of Earth

Figure 20
Banishing Hexagram of Earth

5. Turn to the west. Trace the appropriate Hexagram of Air in the west as you vibrate ARARITA. The upward triangle should be visualized in red and the downward triangle should be visualized in blue.

Figure 21.
Invoking Hexagram of Air

Figure 22
Banishing Hexagram of Air

6. Turn to the north. Trace the appropriate Hexagram of Water in the north as you vibrate ARARITA. The upward triangle should be visualized in red and the downward triangle should be visualized in blue.

Figure 23.
Invoking Hexagram of Water

Figure 24
Banishing Hexagram of Water

7. Return to the east. Repeat the Keyword Analysis and the Signs of LVX.

The Star Ruby and Star Sapphire:

Rather than the Golden Dawn ritual forms, Thelemic magicians may prefer to use the Star Ruby, Aleister Crowley's improved version of the Lesser Ritual of the Pentagram, and the Star Sapphire, which corresponds to the Ritual of the Hexagram. These rituals are not included here but can be found in Crowley's works[4] and also in popular treatments such as Lon Milo Duquette's *"The Magick of Aleister Crowley"*.[5] As the Star Ruby is a banishing ritual and the Star Sapphire is an invoking ritual, together they form an operant field just like the LBRP/LIRH combination.

4. Aleister Crowley, The Book of Lies (York Beach, ME: Weiser Books, 1986) and Magick: Book Four (York Beach, ME: Weiser Books, 1998).
5. Lon Milo DuQuette, The Magick of Aleister Crowley (San Francisco, CA: Weiser Books, 2003).

AOEVEAE ("Stars") Pentagram Ritual:

To replace the Golden Dawn Lesser Ritual of the Pentagram I have developed an Enochian pentagram ritual that I call the AOEVEAE (a-o-i-ve-ah-EH – "stars" in Angelic). A number of writers have come up with Enochian pentagram rituals of this sort and they all share certain similarities. It is pretty clear that the most logical names to use when tracing the pentagrams are the threefold names of God from Dee and Kelley's Great Table (ORO IBAH AOZPI, MPH ARSL GAIOL, OIP TEAA PDOCE, and MOR DIAL HCTGA) and the most logical equivalents to the Archangels are the Kings of the four directions (BATAIVAH, RAAGIOSL, EDLPRNAA, and ICZHIHAL).

Instead of trying to reproduce the Qabalistic Cross like many authors do, I instead begin and end my version of the ritual by tracing the figure of the pentagram across my body accompanied by names from the the central cross portion of the Great Table, known to modern magicians as the Tablet of Union. To me this action embodies the statement in the Lesser Ritual of the Pentagram "About me flames the Pentagram." The ritual begins with the Invoking Pentagram of Active Spirit and ends with the Invoking Pentagram of Passive Spirit, setting up the two basic polarities of the subtle body.

When attributing the names to the directions I use the directional arrangement from the 1587 Tabula Recensa.[6] The text shown here may be adapted to fit the traditional Golden Dawn arrangement of the Great Table by swapping the names associated with the west and south, so that you vibrate OIP TEAA PDOCE in the south and MPH ARSL GAIOL in the west, and swap the directions attributed to RAAGIOSL and EDLPRNAA when calling the Kings.

Start the ritual by standing in the center of your temple facing east, or to the west of the altar facing east if the Holy Table is present. Wear the Enochian PELE ring. If you wish to use a magical weapon, a dagger is probably the most appropriate for the banishing form while a wand is best for the invoking form, but keep in mind that this is a modern practice and Dee and Kelley used neither. The ritual text follows:

1. With your finger or magical weapon, trace from your left hip to your right shoulder while vibrating NANTA

---

6. Lon Milo DuQuette, Enochian Vision Magick (San Francisco, CA: Weiser Books, 2008), 135-137.

(NAHN-ta – Earth), from your right shoulder to left shoulder while vibrating HCOMA (he-KO-ma – Water), from your left shoulder to right hip while vibrating EXARP (EX-arp – Air), from your right hip to your forehead while vibrating BITOM (BI-tom – Fire), and finally from your forehead back to your left hip while vibrating EHNB (EH-nub – Spirit). Then clasp your hands over your heart and vibrate JAIDA (ja-I-da – "The Highest"). Visualize the pentagram traced over your body in bright electric lavender.

Figure 25.
Banishing Pentagram of Earth

2. In the east, trace the Banishing Pentagram of Earth while vibrating ORO IBAH AOZPI. The pentagrams should be visualized as formed from burning flames and as vividly as possible.

3. Turn to the north. In the north, trace the Banishing Pentagram of Earth while vibrating MOR DIAL HCTGA (MOR DI-al hek-TGA).

4. Turn to the west. In the west, trace the Banishing Pentagram of Earth while vibrating OIP TEAA PDOCE (o-IP TE-ah-ah PDO-ke).

5. Turn to the south. In the south, trace the Banishing Pentagram of Earth while vibrating MPH ARSL GAIOL (MEH-peh AR-sal ga-i-OL).

6. Turn back to face the east. Extend your arms to form a cross and vibrate:

RAAS I BATAIVAH
("In the East is BATAIVAH" — ba-ta-i-VAH),

SOBOLN I EDLPRNAA
("In the West is EDLPRNAA" — ed-el-per-na-AH),

BABAGE I RAAGIOSL
("In the South is RAAGIOSL" — ra-AH-gi-oh-sal),

LUCAL I ICZHIHAL
("In the North is ICZHIHAL" — ik-zod-hi-HAL).

7. Make one full spin counter-clockwise while vibrating:

MICMA AO COMSELH AOIVEAE
("Behold the Circle of Stars"
— MIK-ma AH-o KOM-seh-lah a-o-i-ve-a-EH)

Then clasp your hands over your heart while vibrating:

OD OL, MALPRG, NOTHOA
("And I, a Through-Thrusting Fire, in the Midst."
— OD OL, MAL-perg, NOT-ho-ah).

If you are using this ritual in conjunction with the MADRIAX hexagram ritual which follows, it should be inserted here.

8. With your finger or magical weapon, trace from your right hip to your left shoulder while vibrating EHNB, from your left shoulder to your right shoulder while vibrating BITOM, from your right shoulder to left hip while vibrating EXARP, from your left hip to your forehead while vibrating HCOMA, and finally from your forehead back to your

Figure 26.
Invoking Pentagram of Earth

right hip while vibrating NANTA. Then clasp your hands over your heart and vibrate IAIDA. Visualize the pentagram traced over your body in dark, deep purple.

This is the banishing form of the ritual. The invoking form is the same except that the pentagrams should be the Invoking Pentagram of Earth.

In the invoking form, the directional names remain the same but they should be traced to the quarters in clockwise rather than counter-clockwise order. Also, the final spin should be counter-clockwise to align with your initial clockwise rotation.

MADRIAX ("O Ye Heavens") Hexagram Ritual:

To replace the Golden Dawn Lesser Ritual of the Hexagram, I have developed an Enochian hexagram ritual that I call the MADRIAX ("o ye heavens" in Angelic). This ritual has been in development for a long time. I published the original version on the Internet in 2000, and a number of different web sites have archived that version. The 2000 version of this ritual has a number of issues, though I will say that I was still able to get pretty good results with it for a number of years. I've recently rethought various aspects that I think will make it work a lot better based on my ritual findings.

One of the biggest changes is the use of the unicursal hexagram,

Figure 27.
Unicursal Hexagram with Hyperbola

which I have found to work well with the Lesser Ritual of the Hexagram as well. A while back I came across an article by Michael Sanborn[7] that was published on the Internet suggesting that the unicursal hexagram represents the mathematical structure of a hyperbola. In this figure the two rounded curves represent the hyperbola and show how the unicursal hexagram can be mapped onto the figure.

Sanborn goes on to explain that he feels the unicursal hexagram is more elemental than planetary. I will go further — I think that the unicursal hexagram specifically represents the macrocosmic aspect of the elements where they start to "bleed" into the planetary realm. The hyperbola is an excellent representation of the microcosm and macrocosm with one side of the curve representing "above" and the other "below." Overlap the two, as in the unicursal hexagram, and there you have it — an operant field.

Aleister Crowley outlined the elemental associations of the unicursal hexagram in The Book of Thoth. What you do is map the figure onto the Tree of Life centered on Tiphareth, so the upper point on the left side is Fire (Geburah, Mars), the upper point on the right

---

7. Michael Sanborn, The Unicursal Hexagram as Hyperbola (Retrieved 7/5/2011 from http://web. archive.org/web/20040721114312/http://www.xnoubis.org/unicursal.html).

side is Water (Chesed, Jupiter), the lower point on the left side is Air (Hod, Mercury) and the lower point on the right side is Earth (Netzach, Venus). As far as tracing the figure goes for each element, I have adapted the basic Golden Dawn principle that for elemental figures you trace toward the associated point to invoke and away from the associated point to banish. In addition, in keeping with the hyperbola association, you always trace to or away from the top or bottom point. The invoking form may be thought of as bringing the two curves into an overlapping position, while the banishing form may be thought of as separating them back into the normal hyperbola configuration.

In this revised ritual the four elements are attributed to the four quadrants of the Great Table based on the colors from Kelley's original vision of the Watchtowers[8] and the elemental attributions taken from the later "round house" vision[9]. The names vibrated are those of the Kings from the "Heptarchia Mystica":

> Fire = East = BABALEL (Mars)
> Air = South = BNASPOL (Mercury)
> Water = West = BYNEPOR (Jupiter)
> Earth = North = BALIGON (Venus)

If you wish to modify this ritual so as to conform to the zodiacal scheme used in the Golden Dawn Lesser Ritual of the Hexagram you should change these attributions as follows:

> Fire = East = BABALEL (Mars)
> Earth = South = BALIGON (Venus)
> Air = West = BNASPOL (Mercury)
> Water = North = BYNEPOR (Jupiter)

The use of planetary names with the elemental unicursal hexagram represets the union of the planetary and elemental realms, the microcosm and macrocosm. The "above" and "below" points of the ritual are then attributed to BNAPSEN (Saturn) and BLUMAZA (Luna). The figures traced for these points are the usual planetary hexagrams, not the unicursal. When working with the Holy Table the figures form a column running from the heavens to the earth with the hexagram on the Holy Table itself at its midpoint.

8. Meric Causaubon, ed. A True and Faithful Relation of What Passed for Many Years Between Dr. John Dee and Some Spirits (New York, NY: Magickal Childe, 1992), 168.
9. Ibid, 355-361.

Figure 30. Unicursal Hexagram of Air

The final figure used in this ritual is attributed to BOBOGEL (the Sun). It is combined with the invoking unicursal hexagram of Earth to symbolize the invocation and grounding of the solar force. The ritual text is as follows:

1. With your finger or a tool such as a wand trace the Invoking Unicursal Hexagram of Earth over yourself while vibrating BOBOGEL (BO-bo-gel). This tracing is done in the following manner: forehead -> left hip -> right shoulder -> genitals -> left shoulder -> right hip -> forehead. This hexagram is visualized in yellow-gold as opposed to the green that is normally used for elemental earth. It is always traced in the invoking form, even for the banishing form of the ritual.

Figure 28. Invoking Unicursal Hexagram of Earth

2. In the east, trace the invoking unicursal hexagram of Fire in red as you vibrate BABALEL (BA-ba-lel).

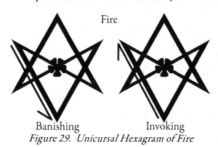

Fire

Banishing   Invoking

Figure 29. Unicursal Hexagram of Fire

3. In the south, trace the invoking unicursal hexagram of Air in white as you vibrate BNASPOL (BNAS-pol).

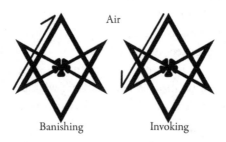

Air

Banishing   Invoking

4. In the west, trace the invoking unicursal hexagram of Water in green as you vibrate BYNEPOR (BY-neh-por).

Banishing   Invoking

Figure 31. Unicursal Hexagram of Water

5. In the north, trace the invoking unicursal hexagram of Earth in black as you vibrate BALIGON (BA-li-gon).

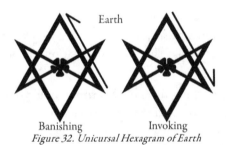

Banishing   Invoking

Figure 32. Unicursal Hexagram of Earth

6. Above you, trace the invoking hexagram of Saturn in bright lavender as you vibrate BNAPSEN (BNAP-sen).

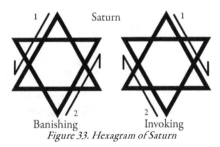

Banishing   Invoking

Figure 33. Hexagram of Saturn

7. Below you, trace the invoking hexagram of the Moon in deep violet as you vibrate BLUMAZA (blu-MA-zah).

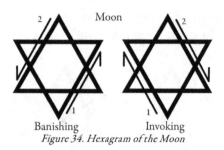

Figure 34. *Hexagram of the Moon*

8. Extend your arms and make one full clockwise rotation (or circumambulation of the temple if you are using the Holy Table) as you vibrate

TA CALZ I OROCHA

(TA CAL-zod I o-RO-ka

— "as above the firmament so beneath you"

(probably the best Enochian rendering of "as above, so below".) Then clasp your hands over your heart for a moment and hold the full visualization of the rite in your mind.

9. For the invoking form of this ritual, hold your hands in front of you with the palms facing outwards and then separate them as though opening a heavy curtain as you vibrate

MADRIAX CARMARA, YOLCAM LONSHI

(MA-dri-ax kar-MA-ra, YOL-cam LON-shi

— "o ye heavens of Carmara, bring forth power".

Carmara is the eighth Heparchial King who rules over the other seven.

10. The ritual work for which you opened the field goes here.

11. At the conclusion of the ritual work, hold your hands in front of you and to either side with palms facing inwards, and then bring them together as though closing a heavy curtain as you vibrate

MADRIAX CARMARA, ADRPAN LONSHI

(MA-dri-ax kar-MA-ra, AH-dra-pan LON-shi

— "o ye heavens of Carmara, cast down power".

This is the invoking form of the ritual. For the banishing form, you would turn to each direction going in a counter-clockwise order (East -> North -> West -> South -> East), trace banishing hexagrams (aside from the opening Earth hexagram which should always be the invoking form), and make the final rotation/circumambulation counter-clockwise.

This ritual works with the AOIVEAE to open and close magical fields just like the Lesser Ritual of the Pentagram/Lesser Ritual of the Hexagram combinations. However, they are designed slightly differently from the other similar rituals found in the tradition in order to streamline magical operations. The main innovation I wanted to incorporate was to encapsulate my workings within both rituals rather than repeating either of them to close down a rite. As a result, the basic structure works like this.

> A. AOIVEAE steps 1 to 7.
> B. MADRIAX steps 1-9.
> C. MADRIAX step 10 is the heptarchial ritual itself.
> D. MADRIAX step 11.
> E. AOIVEAE step 8.

So according to this structure (A) and (B) are the opening, (C) is the ritual work itself, and (D) and (E) constitute the closing. It's an elegant way of doing the ceremonial forms and it is quite fast and efficient once you have the rituals and this structure memorized and get some practice working with it.

The main reason that I developed these rituals was, first of all, to streamline Enochian evocations, and second of all, because I like the idea of matching your ceremonial forms to the magical system that you are using. For Qabalistic rituals I use the LRP/LRH and for Thelemic rituals I use the Star Ruby/Star Sapphire, so I wanted something similar that was directly related to my Enochian work. Truth be told, you can do Enochian work with the Qabalistic or Thelemic rituals, but at least for me matching up the opening rituals to the system works better in terms of objective results.

Devotional Opening Prayers:

While the ceremonial openings have worked well for me over the years, traditional grimoire practitioners may instead want to open the temple in the same manner as Dee and Kelley did when they initially worked with the angels. This devotional method involved a series of prayers directed to the Christian God imploring Him to bless Dee and Kelley that they may enter into communication with the Angels. In addition, even if the temple is opened with ceremonial forms it often works well to add a prayer or devotional element immediately after opening a magical field. The resulting field seems to be more stable and effective, and a devotional element also sets the proper mindset of aspiration leading into the preliminary invocation.

My opinion on Enochian magick and religion is that the two most valid sets of published source material that document genuine angelic conversations and experiences are the Dee diaries themselves and Aleister Crowley's *"The Vision and the Voice"*. As a result, I believe the two religious and philosophical schemas that are most compatible with Enochian work are Hermetic Christianity and Thelema. Dee was a pious adherent of the former system, and Crowley was the founder and prophet of the latter. While this does not necessarily mean that, for example, a Neo-Pagan should expect to encounter difficulties working Enochian magick, what I will say is that if the prayers shown here are used to open the temple they should be made sincerely. In particular, someone who does not believe in the Christian God should not be using Christian prayers. Depending on the circumstances, it may be appropriate for the magician who wishes to use devotional prayers to write his or her own heartfelt devotions and then probability-test the resulting operations to see how well those prayers work.

The Prayer of Enoch:

This prayer was given to Dee and Kelley by the angel Ave on July 7th of 1584 in Krakow.[10] It is the essential devotional prayer used to open the Enochian temple.

> *Lord God the Fountain of true wisdom, thou that openest the secrets thy own self unto man, thou knowest mine imperfection and my inward darknesse:*

---

10. Meric Casaubon, True and Faithful Relation (New York, NY: Magickal Childe, 1992), 196-197.

How can I (therefore) speak unto them that speak not after the voice of man; or worthily call on thy name, considering that my imagination is variable and fruitlesse, and unknown to myself? Shall the Sands seem to invite the Mountains: or can the small Rivers entertain the wonderful and unknown waves? Can the vessel of fear, fragility, or that is of a determined proportion, lift up himself, heave up his hands, or gather the Sun into his bosom?

Lord it cannot be: Lord my imperfection is great: Lord I am lesse than sand: Lord, thy good Angels and Creatures excell me far: our proportion is not alike; our sense agreeth not: Notwithstanding I am comforted; For that we have all one God, all one beginning from thee, that we respect thee a Creatour: Therefore will I call upon thy name, and in thee, I will become mighty. Thou shalt light me, and I will become a Seer; I will see thy Creatures, and will magnifie thee amongst them.

Those that come unto thee have the same gate, and through the same gate, descend, such as thou sendest. Behold, I offer my house, my labour, my heart and soul, If it will please thy Angels to dwell with me, and I with them; to rejoyce with me, that I may rejoyce with them; to minister unto me, that I may magnifie thy name. Then, lo the Tables (which I have provided, and according to thy will, prepared) I offer unto thee, and unto thy holy Angels, desiring them, in and through thy holy names; That as thou art their light, and comfortest them, so they, in thee will be my light and comfort.

Lord they prescribe not laws unto thee, so it is not meet that I prescribe laws unto them; What it pleaseth thee to offer, they receive; So what it pleaseth them to offer unto me, will I also receive. Behold I say (O Lord) If I shall call upon them in thy name, Be it unto me in mercy, as unto the servant of the Highest. Let them also manifest unto me, How, by what words, and at what time, I shall call them. O Lord, Is there any that measure the heavens, that is mortal? How, therefore, can the heavens enter into mans imagination? Thy creatures are the Glory of thy countenance; Hereby thou glorifiest all things, which Glory excelleth and (O Lord) is far above my understanding.

It is great wisdom, to speak and talke according to understanding with Kings; But to command Kings by a subjected commandment, is not wisdom, unlesse it come from thee. Behold Lord, How shall I therefore ascend into the heavens? The air will not carry me, but resisteth my folly, I fall down, for I am of the earth. Therefore, O thou very Light and true Comfort, that canst, and mayst, and dost command the heavens; Behold I offer these Tables unto thee, Command them as it pleaseth thee; and O you Ministers, and true lights of understanding, Governing this earthly frame, and the elements wherein we live, Do for me as for the servant of the Lord; and unto whom it hath pleased the Lord to talk of you.

Behold, Lord, thou hast appointed me 50 times; Thrice 50 times will I lift my hands unto thee. Be it unto me as it pleaseth thee, and thy holy Ministers. I require nothing but thee, and through thee, and for thy honour and glory; But I hope I shall be satisfied, and shall not die, (as thou hast promised) until thou gather the clouds together, and judge all things; when in a moment I shall be changed and dwell with thee for ever. Amen.

While Dee approached this text as a Christian prayer it is generic enough to be employed by Thelemites and has the added legitimacy of originating with the Angelic communications themselves, unlike the other opening prayers which were written by Dee and thus are more open to revision. From a Thelemic perspective, the second paragraph may seem problematic with its references to the unworthiness of the magician and so forth, but the overall spirit of the paragraph is more in keeping with the vision of the individual that is common to both Gnostic Christianity and Thelema — that the realization of the divine spark overcomes this initial unworthiness, whether it be envisioned as the grace of God or the True Will of the magician. For example, some similar statements may be found in the Confession that begins Crowley's Invocation of Horus, also called *The Supreme Ritual* by Thelemites and which is believed to have ushered in the New Aeon when it was performed in 1904.

Chapter 8
Preliminary Invocation

*T*he preliminary invocations follow the ceremonial and/or devotional temple openings. While the devotional prayers articulate your aspiration as a magician, the essential function of this ritual phase is to align your personal consciousness with that of deity — in effect, to transform you into an instrument of God for the duration of the ritual. It should also serve to energize your subtle body and align it with the magical forces that you will be calling upon during the course of the ritual.

NAZ OLPIRT ("Pillars of Light") Energy Work Exercise:

While this is a modern practice of my own design that is not found in the Dee material, I have found it to be quite effective like the ceremonial opening rituals. Also as with the ceremonial rituals, it should be memorized rather than read, and better still performed as part of a regular daily ritual practice. Daily ritual practice is like the magical equivalent of working out. The more you do it, the stronger you get, and the more regularly you practice the better. I would recommend a practice consisting of the AOEVEAE and this exercise to start out, and once you feel comfortable with that sequence you can add the MADRIAX as well to extend the effect of the practice into the macrocosmic realm.

One of the areas that modern magicians sometimes neglect is the energetic state of the subtle body, or body of light. I have found that practices such as Hatha Yoga and Qigong make a great deal of difference in terms of the amount of magical force you can bring to bear upon a situation and thus your ability to create change successfully. In the Golden Dawn tradition, a common practice is the *Middle Pillar Exercise*, which associates various names of God with specific points on the subtle body and as a result empowers those areas with the energies of the associated godforms. In the Thelemic tradition, a similar practice is the *Elevenfold Seal*, found in Aleister Crowley's *"Liber V vel Reguli"*.

This is a similar exercise based upon relating the Enochian elements to the elemental natures of the seven chakras of Eastern mysticism. While no scientific research has as of yet identified chakras or the meridians that connect them on the human body, traditional Chinese medicine has made use of them for millennia in treating various illnesses through practices such as acupuncture, which produces remarkable results for many people. This ritual activates these energy circuits using the magical force of the Enochian elements and aligns the body of light with the magical currents of the Enochian system.

Start off by standing in a normal, relaxed pose. Keep your spine straight and imagine your head suspended by a thread from above. Breathe slowly and easily through the nose into your diaphragm. Place your tongue so that it is touching the roof of your mouth and keep it there except when vibrating the words of the ritual. Make sure you hold the tongue in that position when breathing in. The gestures are made with the hand or finger rather than any sort of magical weapon.

1. Make a clockwise circle above your head and intone:
    MADRIAX
    ("the Heavens")
    three times. Visualize a sea of luminous brilliance above you, beyond and encompassing all colors.

2. Touch the center of your forehead (ajna chakra) and intone:

IAD

(i-AHD – "God")

three times. Visualize energy akin to pure, clear light forming at this point, sending its rays outward to the four cardinal directions. Do not completely drop the visualization of luminous brilliance above you. You are adding to your visualization, not replacing it. This instruction holds true for all the following steps.

3. Touch your throat (vishuddha chakra) and intone:

EHNB

("Spirit")

three times. Visualize a sphere of bright lavender light forming at this point.

4. Touch the center of your chest (anahata chakra) and intone:

EXARP

("Air")

three times. Visualize a sphere of vibrant white energy forming at this point.

5. Touch your solar plexus (samsara chakra) and intone:

BITOM

("Fire")

three times. Visualize a sphere of glowing red energy forming at this point.

6. Touch the lower abdomen just below the navel (svadasthana chakra) and intone:

HCOMA

("Water")

three times. Visualize a sphere of green energy forming at this point.

7. Touch the perineum (muladhara chakra) and intone:

NANTA

("Earth")

three times. Visualize a sphere of solid black energy forming at this point.

8. Drop both hands to your sides and intone:

CAOSGO

(ka-OS-go – "the Earth")

three times. Visualize the completion of a circuit that begins above you in the heavens, descends below you into the deep earth down the front of your body and then ascends upwards to the heavens along the back of your body.

9. As you visualize the circulating energy, start with your hands at about the level of your perineum, palms turned upwards, and then raise them to the level of the top of your head as you inhale. Then turn the palms downward and drop them back to the level of the perineum as you exhale. This breathing should be deep, relaxed, and as smooth as possible. When performed properly you should feel a light tingling sensation up and down the spine that roughly follows your hand motions. Hold this visualization of the energy circuit in concert with your breathing for as long as is comfortable or appropriate.

10. To conclude the exercise, make the Sign of Osiris Risen, crossing your arms over your chest, and intone:

TA CALZ I OROCHA

("As above the firmament so beneath you")

as you visualize any excess energy you have focused at each of the points of your body descending below your feet into the vast darkness of the deep earth, breaking the circuit. Feel a wave of relaxation sweep over you from your head down to your feet, sweeping any remaining tension into the deep earth along with the grounded energy.

Even though the *"Heptarchia Mystica"* relies on the agency of particular angels in order to accomplish magical objectives, I have found that this sort of "energy work" nonetheless plays an important role in obtaining the best possible magical results. While modern magicians continue to debate the "energy model" versus the "spirit model" of magick, in my experience this is a false dichotomy. When a

84

magician conjures a spirit to accomplish a particular task, the magical result depends on both the power of the spirit and that of the magician, which merge together to produce the desired effect.

John Dee's Oration to God:

This opening prayer serves as the preliminary invocation for rituals summoning the Heptarchial Kings and Princes. It explains his purpose for working magick and implores the favor of his deity. The text of the prayer shows the extent of Dee's Christian faith and its Hermetic influences, which included the belief that an individual could, through extreme devotion, communicate directly with the divine.

> *O Almighty, Aeternal, the True and Living God; O King of Glory, O Lord of Hosts, O Thou, the Creator of Heaven and Earth, and of all things, visible and invisible; Now, (even now, at length) among other Thy manifold mercies used, and to be used toward me, Thy simple servant, [John Dee][1], I most humbly beseech Thee, in this my present petition to have mercy upon me, to have pity upon me, to have compassion upon me. I, faithfully and sincerely, of long time, have sought among men, in Earth, and also by prayer (full oft and pitifully) have made suit unto Thy Divine Majesty for the obtaining of some convenient portion of True Knowledge and Understanding of Thy laws and ordinances, established in the natures and properties of Thy creatures; by which Knowledge, Thy Divine Wisdom, Power and Goodness, (on Thy creatures bestowed and to them imparted), being to me made and allure me, (for the same) incessantly to pronounce Thy praises, to render unto Thee, most hearty thanks, to advance Thy true honor, and to win unto Thy Name, some of Thy due Majestic Glory, among all people, and forever.*

> *And, whereas it hath pleased Thee (O God) of Thy Infinite Goodness, by Thy faithful and holy Spiritual Messengers, to deliver unto me, long since*

---

1. Obviously you would insert your own name or magical motto here. You may want to make a note of this in the margin so that you do not inadvertently use Dee's name during a ritual rather than your own.

(through the eye and ear of E. K.)[2] *an orderly form, and manner of exercise Heptarchial; How, (to Thy Honour and Glory, and the Comfort of my own poor soul, and of others, Thy faithful servants,) I may, at all times, use very many of Thy good Angels, their counsels and helps; according to the properties of such their functions, and offices, as to them, by Thy Divine Power, Wisdom and Goodness, is assigned, and limited; (Which orderly form, and manner of exercise, until even now, I never found opportunity and extreme necessity, to apply myself unto.)*

Therefore, I Thy poor, and simple servant, do most humbly, heartily, and faithfully beseech Thy Divine Majesty, most lovingly and fatherly to favour; and by Thy Divine Beck to further this my present industry and endeavour to exercise myself, according to the foresaid orderly form and manner; And, now, (at length, but not too late) for Thy dearly beloved Son Jesus Christ His sake, (O Heavenly Father) to grant also unto me, this blessing and portion of Thy heavenly Graces; that Thou wilt forthwith, enable me, make me apt and acceptable, (in body, soul, and spirit) to enjoy always the holy and friendly conversation, with the sensible, plain, full, and perfect help, in word and deed, of Thy Mighty, Wise, and Good Spiritual Messengers and Ministers generally; and, namely, of Blessed Michael, Blessed Gabriel, Blessed Raphael, and Blessed Uriel; and also especially, of all those, which do appertain unto the Heptarchial Mystery, theurgically (as yet) and very briefly unto me declared; under the method of the Seven Mighty Kings, and their Seven Faithful and Princely Ministers, with their subjects and servants, to them belonging.

And in this Thy Great Mercy and Grace, on me bestowed, and to me confirmed, (O Almighty God)

---

2. Also, if you are working with a scryer his or her name should be placed here. If working alone you can amend it to "through my own eye and ear" or omit the parenthesized portion entirely.

Thou shalt, (to the great comfort of Thy faithful servants,) approve, to Thy very enemies, and mine, the truth and certainty of Thy manifold, most merciful promises, heretofore, made unto me: And that Thou art the True and Almighty God, Creator of Heaven and Earth, (upon whom I do call and in whom I put all of my trust,) and Thy Ministers, to be the true, and faithful Angels of Light; which have, hitherto, principally, and according to Thy Divine providence dealt with us; And, also, I thy poor and simple servant, shall then, In and By Thee, be better able to serve Thee, according to Thy well pleasing; to Thy Honour and Glory; Yea, even in these most miserable, and lamentable days. Grant, Oh grant, O our heavenly father, grant this, (I pray Thee,) for Thy only begotten Son Jesus Christ His sake: Amen, Amen, Amen.

Revised Oration to God:

This revised version was developed by my magical working group to harmonize better with the Thelemic worldview. Much of the text is the same, but it is shorter and does not include the original's explicitly Christian material.

O Almighty, Eternal, True and Living God; O King of Glory; O Lord of Hosts; O Thou, who art Heaven and Earth and all things visible and invisible; we beseech Thee in this our present petition to have mercy and compassion upon us, who, faithfully and sincerely of long time have made suit unto Thy Divine Majesty, that we may obtain true Gnosis and full understanding of Thy Divine Wisdom, Power and Goodness. And whereas it has pleased Thee of Thy infinite Goodness, by Thy faithful and holy Spiritual Messengers, to deliver unto us long since an orderly form and manner of Exercise Angelic: how, to Thy Honor and Glory, and the comfort of our own souls and of others Thy faithful servants, we may at all times use very many of Thy Holy Angels, their counsels and helps: according to the properties of such their functions and offices, as to them, by Thy Divine Power, Wisdom and Goodness is assigned and limited. Therefore, we heartily and faithfully beseech Thy Divine Majesty to further this our present industry and endeavor to Exercise ourselves, according to the aforesaid orderly form and manner. Grant also unto us this blessing and portion of Thy Heavenly Graces: that thou wilt forthwith enable us, make us apt, and acceptable in body, Soul, and Spirit to enjoy always the Holy and friendly conversation, with the sensible, plain, full and perfect help in word and deed of Thy Mighty, Wise and Good Spiritual Messengers and Ministers generally: and namely of Blessed Michael, Blessed Gabriel, Blessed Raphael and Blessed Uriel; and also, especially of all those which do appertain unto the Heptarchical Mystery and the Mystery of the Great Table. Reveal unto us Thy Majestical Glory, now and forever, through Thy Ministers, the true and faithful Angels of Light. AMEN. AMEN. AMEN.

Daily Magical Practice:

Some traditional grimoire practitioners have recently put forth the argument that since the old grimoires do not specify any sort of daily magical practice such work is not necessary for working successful magick. I strongly disagree with this assertion, and in my experience there is no surer way to fail as a magician than to neglect daily practice. Even if you possess profound magical talent, daily practices will make your rituals even more effective, just as professional athletes have to maintain their workout schedules in order to remain in top shape.

In fact, the *"Heptarchia Mystica"* as written does include a daily practice — the threefold repetition of the Oration to God as a prayer.[3] In my opinion this prayer should be preceded by opening an operant field and performing the NAZ OLPIRT or similar exercise such as the *Elevenfold Seal* or *Middle Pillar*, and then followed by a period of silent meditation, but these are modern additions on my part. For traditional

---

3. Geoffrey James, Enochian Evocation (Berkeley Heights, NJ: Heptangle, 1984), 53.

grimoire practitioners who would rather not employ such forms, the repetition of the prayer is still quite effective on its own. Furthermore, it would not surprise me if Dee himself did in fact observe a period of silent meditation following his prayers, but failed to note it in the text of his grimoire because he found the practice obvious. Twenty minutes or more of meditation per day is excellent if you can find the time for it, but even five minutes is better than none.

In addition to strengthening your magical abilities, employing the same essential procedure that you use to open the temple in your daily work will allow you to memorize the rituals that make up the opening procedure much more quickly. The Oration itself is likely intended to be read like the other texts in the Enochian system, but the ceremonial rituals should be commited to memory as they are rather awkward to perform while holding a book or script and include visualizations that can easily be disrupted by shifting your attention back to the printed page.

Scott Michael Stenwick

Chapter 9
The Angelic Keys

The Angelic Keys, or *Calls*, make up what is probably the most famous portion of the Enochian system. It is from the Keys and their English translations that all "Enochian dictionaries" are created; in fact, the Keys make up the only portion of the system where the English and Angelic languages appear side by side. There are forty-nine actual Keys — the eighteen Keys attributed to the Tablet of the Watchtowers, the thirty Keys attributed to the Aires (which differ from one another by only the name of the Aire), and the mysterious true "First Key" that precedes the other forty-eight. I divide the Keys into three groups: the Opening Keys, used to open and close the Temple, the Watchtower Keys, which correspond to the various regions of the Great Table, and the Aethyr Keys, which correspond to the thirty Aires.

The use of Angelic Keys with the rituals of the *Heptarchia Mystica* is not noted anywhere in the grimoire itself, and it is for this reason that I have noted it as an optional practice in the ritual template. Based on years of workings with my magical group, however, I have found this innovation to be quite effective. As the heptarchial Kings and Princes are not attributed to the Great Table or Aires it is only the Opening Keys that are appropriate for use with these entities, and for this reason only these of Keys are included in this chapter.

The Opening Keys

Silence – the True "First Key":

While many versions of the Keys have been published, one obscure piece of related information is that there are 49 Keys rather than 48. When the Keys were communicated to Dee and Kelly they were told that the true First Key was "not to be sounded." Some authors have interpreted this to mean that the use of this Key was forbidden in some manner, but my own interpretation is that the true First Key does not consist of words and is therefore silent. From a philosophical point of view, this is akin to the notion that stillness of mind, not just physical silence, is a requirement preceding any successful magical action. Prior to reading any of the Angelic Keys, I perform a brief meditation lasting a few minutes that serves to quiet any remaining wandering thoughts.

The First Key:

As I have discussed above, the "First Key" is actually the second, but I have not labeled it as such in order to maintain consistency with other writings on Enochian Magick. It is also worth noting that the Angels used the same sort of notation when communicating with Dee and Kelly; while they acknowledged that the First Key was really the Second, they continued to refer to it as the First in their subsequent communications. The First Key is used to activate the Enochian Temple when performing rituals involving evocation — that is, the calling of Enochian Angels into the Holy Table. As an opening Key, it precedes the use of all Watchtower or Aethyr Keys.

The Second Key:

> The Second Key is used to open the Enochian temple for rituals involving invocation — that is, the calling of Enochian Angels into body and consciousness of the magician. Invocation and evocation are not necessarily contradictory; for example, I have been known to perform rituals in which I invoked the form of a particular Angel in order to call a second Angel into the Holy Table that was under the authority of the first. Also, there are many cases in which a spell is intended to have an effect on both the magician and his or her external environment. For such rituals both Keys are read beginning with the First. Otherwise, in the case of a ritual involving invocation only, the Second Key replaces the First.

The First and Second Keys follow. They are shown in Angelic, which translates the actual Angelic letters of the Keys into their English alphabet equivalents; Phonetic, which breaks the pronunciation down by syllable according to the pronunciation explained in Chapter 4; and English, the translation of the Angelic. I have decided not to arrange them in such a way as to provide a word by word comparison between the English and Angelic as many Enochian books do simply because I find that the format used here is more usable in ritual. If you are interested in studying the language itself several Enochian Dictionaries are available for that purpose. The most popular of these among practitioners is probably *The Complete Enochian Dictionary* by Donald C. Laycock, available from Weiser Books[1].

---

1. Donald C. Laycock, The Complete Enochian Dictionary (York Beach, ME: Weiser Books, 2001).

The First Angelic Key

OL SONF VORSG, GOHO IAD BALT LANSH CALZ
VONPHO, SOBRA Z-OL ROR I TA NAZPSAD GRAA TA
MALPRG. DS HOL-Q QAA NOTHOA ZIMZ OD COMMAH
TA NOBLOH ZIEN: SOBA THIL GNONP PRGE ALDI DS
VRBS OBOLEH GRSAM: CASARM OHORELA CABA PIR DS
ZONRENSG CAB ERM JADNAH: PILAH FARZM ZURZA
ADNA GONO IADPIL DS HOM TOH SOBA IPAM LU IPAMIS
DS LOHOLO VEP ZOMD POAMAL OD BOGPA AAI TA PIAP
PIAMOL OD VAOAN. ZACARE CA OD ZAMRAN ODO CICLE
QAA ZORGE, LAP ZIRDO NOCO MAD HOATH JAIDA.

Phonetic

OL SONF VORSG go-HO i-AD BALT LANSH KALZ VON-
pho, SO-bra zod-OL ROR I TA NAZ-psad GRA-a TA MAL-perg.
DES HOL-quo QUA-a not-HO-a ZIMZ, OD KO-mah TA NO-bloh
zi-EN: SO-ba THIL gi-NONP per-GE AL-di DES VURBS O-bu-leh
gir-SAM: ka-SARM o-ho-RE-la ka-BA PIR DES zon-RENSG KAB
ERM JAHD-na: PE-lah FARZM OD ZUR-za ad-NA GO-no i-AHD-
pil DES HOM TOH SO-ba i-PAM LU i-PAHM-is, DES LO-huh-lo
VEP ZOMD po-A-mal OD BOG-pa ah-uh-I TA pi-AP pi-A-mol OD
VA-o-an. za-ka-REH KA OD ZAM-ran: O-do kik-LEH QUA-a zor-
GEH, LAP ZIR-do NO-ko MAD ho-ATH ja-I-da.

English

I reign over you, sayeth the God of Justice in power exalted above
the firmaments of wrath, in whose hands the Sun is as a sword, and the
Moon as a through-thrusting fire which measureth your garments in
the midst of my vestures, and trussed you together as the palms of my
hands: whose seats I garnished with the fire of gathering, and beautified
your garments with admiration to whom I made a law to govern
the Holy Ones and delivered you a rod with the Ark of Knowledge.
Moreover you lifted up your voices and swore obedience and faith to
him that liveth and triumpheth whose beginning is not, nor end cannot
be which shineth as a flame in the midst of your palace and reigneth
among you as the balance of righteousness, and truth: move, therefore,

and show yourselves: open the mysteries of your creation: be friendly unto me: for I am the servant of the same your God: the true worshipper of the highest.

The Second Angelic Key

ADGT VPAAH ZONGOM FAAIP SALD VIIV L SOBAM IALPRG IZAZAZ PIADPH CASARMA ABRAMG TA TALHO PARACLEDA Q-TA LORS-L-Q TURBS OOGE BALTOH GIUI CHIS LUSD ORRI OD MICALP CHIS BIA OZONGON. LAP NOAN TROF CORS TAGE O-Q MANIN JAIDON. TORZU GOHEL ZACAR CA CNOQUOD, ZAMRAN MICALZO OD OZAZM VRELP LAP ZIR IOIAD.

Phonetic

AD-git VEH-puh-a ZONG-om fa-uh-IP SALD VI-iv LA so-BAM i-AL-perg i-zuh-ZAZ pi-AD-peh, kas-AR-ma ab-RAMG TA TAL-ho pa-ruh-KLEH-da QUO-ta LORS-el-quo TURBS O-uh-ge BAL-toh gi-u-I CHIS OR-ri OD mi-KALP CHIS bi-A O-zun-gon. LAP no-AN TROF KORS ta-GE O-quo ma-NIN JA-i-don tor-ZU GO-hel za-KAR KA KNO-quod, ZAM-ran mi-KAL-zo OD o-ZA-zam VRELP LAP ZIR i-O-i-ad.

English

Can the wings of the winds understand your voices of wonder, O you the second of the first, whom the burning flames have framed within the depths of my jaws, whom I have prepared as cups for a wedding, or as the flowers in their beauty for the chamber of righteousness. Stronger are your feet than the barren stone: and mightier are your voices than the manifold winds. For, you are become a building such as is not but in the mind of the all-powerful. Arise, sayeth the first, move therefore unto his servants: show yourselves in power. And make me a strong seething: for I am of him that liveth forever.

Chapter 10
Tuning the Space

Once the general preliminary invocation has been performed, the next step in the ritual is to tune the working space to match the attribution of the spirit that is to be conjured. The function of this step is to create a magical environment that will be favorable to both the spirit being conjured and the desired outcome of the ritual.

Planetary Days and Hours:

Renaissance magicians relied on planetary days and hours to tune their ritual spaces, working with the natural sequence of planetary influences rather than any particular ceremonial procedure. The planetary days follow the standard Western attributions for the days of the week:

Sunday = Sun
Monday = Moon
Tuesday = Mars
Wednesday = Mercury
Thursday = Jupiter
Friday = Venus
Saturday = Saturn

Figuring out the planetary hour is somewhat more involved. Each day begins at sunrise with the first hour of the day. The time from sunrise to sunset is then divided into twelve equal parts, which are the hours of the day. The time from sunset to sunrise is then likewise divided into twelve equal parts, which are the twelve hours of the night. This means that the amount of time allotted to the hours of the day and hours of the night will only be equal on the equinoxes – the hours of the day will be longer in summer and the hours of the night will be longer in winter.

For example:

if sunrise is at	7:03 AM
and sunset is at	5:50 PM,

the time between sunrise and sunset is: 10 hours and 47 minutes or 647 minutes. Dividing 647 by 12 and rounding to the nearest minute gives 54 minutes, which will be the length of each hour of the day.

The first hour starts at 7:03 AM, the second 54 minutes later at 7:57 AM, and so forth. Since there are 1440 minutes in a 24 hour day, there are 793 minutes between sunset and the following sunrise. Dividing 793 by 12 and rounding to the nearest minute gives 66 minutes for each hour of the night. The first night hour would begin at 5:50 PM, the second would begin 66 minutes later at 6:56 PM, and so forth. The length of one day hour plus the length of one night hour should always sum to 120 minutes.

The planets are then attributed to the hours using an arrangement called the Chaldean Order. This is the order of apparent astrological motion from the perspective of the Earth, and also the descending order of the planets on the Tree of Life — Saturn, Jupiter, Mars, Sun, Venus, Mercury, and finally Moon. The first hour of the day is always ruled by the planet that rules the day, and subsequent hours are ruled by the planets next in order. Once all seven ancient planets are attributed to hours the sequence starts over. It is important to note that Renaissance magicians considered the planetary hour to be more important than the planetary day, which allowed them to work planetary magick on any day of the week as circumstances required.

Table 5: Planetary Hours of the Day – Sunrise to Sunset

	Sunday	Monday	Tuesday	Wednesday	Thursday	Friday	Saturday
1	Sun	Moon	Mars	Mercury	Jupiter	Venus	Saturn
2	Venus	Saturn	Sun	Moon	Mars	Mercury	Jupiter
3	Mercury	Jupiter	Venus	Saturn	Sun	Moon	Mars
4	Moon	Mars	Mercury	Jupiter	Venus	Saturn	Sun
5	Saturn	Sun	Moon	Mars	Mercury	Jupiter	Venus
6	Jupiter	Venus	Saturn	Sun	Moon	Mars	Mercury
7	Mars	Mercury	Jupiter	Venus	Saturn	Sun	Moon
8	Sun	Moon	Mars	Mercury	Jupiter	Venus	Saturn
9	Venus	Saturn	Sun	Moon	Mars	Mercury	Jupiter
10	Mercury	Jupiter	Venus	Saturn	Sun	Moon	Mars
11	Moon	Mars	Mercury	Jupiter	Venus	Saturn	Sun
12	Saturn	Sun	Moon	Mars	Mercury	Jupiter	Venus

Table 6: Planetary Hours of the Night – Sunset to Sunrise

	Sunday	Monday	Tuesday	Wednesday	Thursday	Friday	Saturday
1	Jupiter	Venus	Saturn	Sun	Moon	Mars	Mercury
2	Mars	Mercury	Jupiter	Venus	Saturn	Sun	Moon
3	Sun	Moon	Mars	Mercury	Jupiter	Venus	Saturn
4	Venus	Saturn	Sun	Moon	Mars	Mercury	Jupiter
5	Mercury	Jupiter	Venus	Saturn	Sun	Moon	Mars
6	Moon	Mars	Mercury	Jupiter	Venus	Saturn	Sun
7	Saturn	Sun	Moon	Mars	Mercury	Jupiter	Venus
8	Jupiter	Venus	Saturn	Sun	Moon	Mars	Mercury
9	Mars	Mercury	Jupiter	Venus	Saturn	Sun	Moon
10	Sun	Moon	Mars	Mercury	Jupiter	Venus	Saturn
11	Venus	Saturn	Sun	Moon	Mars	Mercury	Jupiter
12	Mercury	Jupiter	Venus	Saturn	Sun	Moon	Mars

These tables show the arrangement of the planetary hours for the day and night. The most efficacious time to perform a standard planetary ritual is on the day and hour of the planet. Such a solar ritual would thus be most effective when performed on a Sunday during the first or eighth hour of the day or the third or tenth hour of the night, since those hours are attributed to the Sun on every Sunday.

When working with the *Mystical Heptarchy* it is necessary to work during the proper planetary day. John Dee further notes planetary attributions for each King and Prince, which specify the planetary hour in which they are to be conjured. The attributions of the Kings all match the planetary days, so that for example Bobogel, the King for Sunday, should be conjured during the day and hour of the Sun. The Princes are summoned during different planetary hours, such that Bornogo, the Prince for Sunday, should be conjured on the day of the Sun but during the hour of Venus.

Dee noted that while the King and Prince rule for the entire day, the Ministers associated with them rule according to the "six parts of the day." Presumably this means that the day should be divided into six groups of four planetary hours each starting at sunrise, three for the day followed by three for the night. As there are no conjurations in the "Heptarchia Mystica" specific to the Ministers, this notation seems to be of little practical use in the context of the original system. However, this does present an area of the heptarchial system that has not yet been explored and thus could prove fruitful for further magical research.

Incense:

Many systems of evocation involve the use of incense that the conjured spirit uses to shape a rudimentary form for the magician to observe. There are no explicit references in the Dee diaries to the use of any particular incense, and it is not clear that any was ever used. Kelley viewed the spirits in a scrying stone rather than seeing them appear in patterns of smoke. However, if you wish to use incense in a heptarchial ritual the proper type is that corresponding to the planetary day. This is the case even if you are evoking the Prince, whose planetary hour differs from the planetary day, or Carmara and Hagonel, who adapt to the day on which they are conjured. Some incenses corresponding to the seven planets and days of the week according to Aleister Crowley's "*Liber 777*" (column XLII) are as follows:

Sunday: Olibanum, Cinnamon, all glorious odors.

Monday: Jasmine, Camphor, Aloe, all sweet virginal odors.

Tuesday: Tobacco, Pepper, Dragon's Blood, all hot pungent odors.

Wednesday: Mastic, White Sandal, Nutmeg, Mace, Storax, all fugitive odors.

Thursday: Cedar, Saffron, all generous odors.

Friday: Benzoin, Rose, Red Sandal, Sandalwood, Myrtle, all soft voluptuous odors.

Saturday: Myrhh, Civet, Assofoetida, Scammony, Indigo, Sulphur, all evil odors.

As one of the functions of incense is to prompt particular impressions in the mind, it is important to note that the italicized descriptions in the list above are essentially subjective. For example, a "glorious odor" would be incense that calls to mind a sense of glory or exaltation. This is difficult to codify and depends upon the way in which your consciousness responds to particular scents, so these general descriptions are included to accommodate such individual differences.

There are no specific instructions in the Dee diaries regarding the construction or placement of an incense burner, but my magical working group has found that one may be set on the Holy Table without causing any functional problems. Just make sure that the burner you use does not heat up too much on the bottom or it can singe the silk of the cloth.

Ceremonial Forms:

Rather than working with the system of planetary days and hours many modern magicians rely on ceremonial forms to tune the ritual space. The most common such ritual for planetary operations is the Golden Dawn *Greater Invoking Ritual of the Hexagram*. When working with the mystical heptarchy it is my practice to conjure during the proper day and hour and also use the ceremonial forms to tune the space, but Dee himself most likely relied on the days and hours as specified in Agrippa's *"Three Books of Occult Philosophy"* so the use of the hexagram ritual is marked as optional in the template for those traditional magicians who would rather work without using the modern forms.

The *Greater Invoking Ritual of the Hexagram* is performed by tracing the proper invoking planetary hexagram and symbol to each of the four quarters of the temple beginning in the east and rotating deosil, or clockwise. The formula ARARITA is vibrated while tracing the hexagram and the name of God corresponding to the planet is vibrated while tracing the symbol in the center of the hexagram. The hexagram should be visualized in the natural color corresponding to the planet, while the symbol should be visualized in the flashing or complementary color. So, for example, when performing the *Greater Invoking Hexagram of Mars* the hexagram should be visualized in red and the symbol of Mars should be visualized in green.

This is further complicated by the type of operation being performed. For a ritual seeking knowledge or realization the natural color for the sphere of the planet should be used, whereas for a ritual conjuring a particular magical power the natural color for the path of the planet should be used. On the Tree of Life the sphere of the planet represents its intelligence or consciousness while the path of planet represents its spirit or activity. The name of God remains the same whether you are working with a sphere or a path, but the natural color shifts or changes as shown on the following table.

Table 7. Planetary Attributions

Planet	Name of God	Sphere Color	Path Color
Saturn	YHVH Elohim	Black	Indigo
Jupiter	Al or El	Blue	Purple
Mars	Elohim Gibor	Scarlet Red	Scarlet
Sun	YHVH Eloah ve-Da'ath	Yellow or Gold	Orange
Venus	YHVH Tzabaoth	Emerald Green	Emerald
Mercury	Elohim Tzabaoth	Orange	Yellow
Moon	Shaddai el Chai	Violet	Blue

As the Kings generally are conjured for knowledge, it is usually most appropriate to use the Sphere color when summoning them. As the Princes generally are conjured to perform some particular task, it is usually most appropriate to use the Path color when summoning them. However, there are some exceptions to this rule and the goal of the operation should be the final arbiter of which color is most appropriate.

The planetary hexagrams follow. The general methodology used is to map the planetary hexagram onto the Tree of Life so that the planets are attributed as shown. Then you begin tracing at the appropriate point and trace clockwise to invoke. These hexagrams can also be used to banish by starting at the planetary point and tracing counter-clockwise.

Figure 35. Planetary Hexagram

The one exception to this basic rule is the Hexagram of the Sun. Since the Sun is located in the center of the planetary hexagram there is no point to attribute to it. Therefore, in order to invoke the Sun, the other six hexagrams are traced in order according to relative astrological motion: Saturn, Jupiter, Mars, Venus, Mercury, and finally the Moon. The figure is then traced in the complementary color at the center of the figure as the name of God YHVH Eloah ve-Da'ath is vibrated once.

Saturn

Banishing   Invoking

Figure 36. Hexagram of Saturn

For the sphere of Saturn the hexagram is traced in black and the central symbol is traced in white. For the path of Saturn the hexagram is traced in indigo and the central symbol is traced in light yellow.

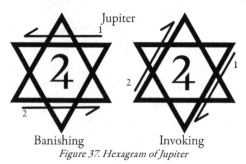

Jupiter

Banishing   Invoking

Figure 37. Hexagram of Jupiter

For the sphere of Jupiter the hexagram is traced in blue and the central symbol is traced in orange. For the path of Jupiter the hexagram is traced in purple and the central symbol is traced in yellow.

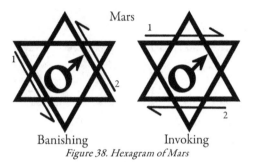

Mars

Banishing   Invoking
Figure 38. Hexagram of Mars

For the sphere of Mars the hexagram is traced in scarlet red and the central symbol is traced in green. For the path of Mars the hexagram is traced in scarlet and the central symbol is traced in light green.

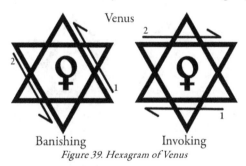

Venus

Banishing   Invoking
Figure 39. Hexagram of Venus

For the sphere of Venus the hexagram is traced in emerald green and the central symbol is traced in red. For the path of Venus the hexagram is traced in emerald and the central symbol is traced in light red.

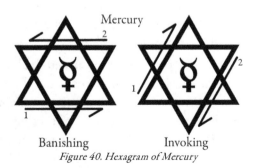

Mercury

Banishing   Invoking
Figure 40. Hexagram of Mercury

For the sphere of Mercury the hexagram is traced in orange and the central symbol is traced in blue. For the path of Mercury the hexagram is traced in yellow and the central symbol is traced in purple.

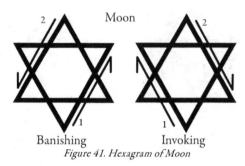

Figure 41. Hexagram of Moon

For the sphere of the Moon the hexagram is traced in violet and the central symbol is traced in pale yellow. For the path of the Moon the hexagram is traced in blue and the central symbol is traced in orange.

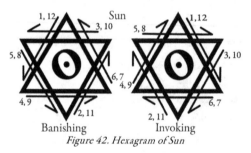

Figure 42. Hexagram of Sun

The hexagram of the Sun is an amalgam of the other planetary hexagrams and is traced by superimposing them over one another. ARARITA is vibrated six times, once for each hexagram traced, but the godname is only vibrated once along with the symbol.

For the sphere of the Sun the hexagrams are traced in yellow or gold and the central symbol is traced in purple. For the path of the Sun the hexagrams are traced in orange and the central symbol is traced in blue.

Finally, once the hexagrams have been traced to all four quarters, the Greater Ritual of the Hexagram is concluded by turning back to face the east and raising your wand or finger to the heavens. You then exclaim "let the divine light descend!" and bring your wand or finger down in a vertical line until reaches the working space on the altar. When working with the mystical heptarchy this will be the center of the Sigillum Dei Aemeth. The accompanying visualization for the invoking form is a column of light matching the color used for the hexagram descending from the heavens and coming to rest in the center of the working space. For the banishing form, rather than the light coming to rest in the center it should instead be visualized as filling the temple space and then fading as it purifies the working area of the specified planetary influence. Generally speaking, you will be using the invoking form when working with heptarchial Kings and Princes, as they are dismissed using the License to Depart rather than the banishing form of this ritual.

Chapter 11
Heptarchial Conjurations

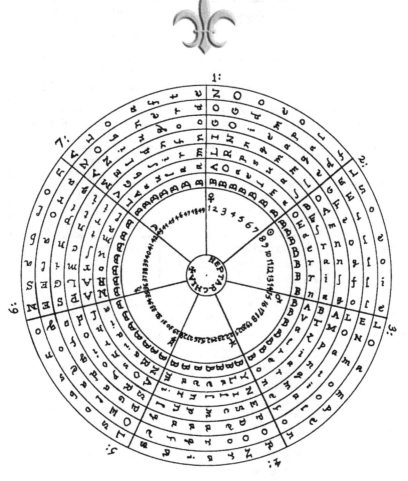

Figure 43.
The Heptarchial wheel showing the Kings, Princes, and Ministers

*O*nce the space has been tuned by day and hour or the Greater Ritual of the Hexagram, or both, to the appropriate planetary influence, the magician may proceed with the conjuration of the desired King or Prince. Compared to many other systems of magick, the method found in the *"Heptarchia Mystica"* is a relatively straightforward procedure. While assembling the various temple implements can be a lot of work, once you have them in place summoning the Kings and Princes is quite simple.

King	Conjuration Powers	Traditional Powers
Carmara	Dispensing and governing the heptarchial doctrine.	Vision of the Machinery of the Universe
Bobogel	Distributing, giving, and bestowing wisdom and science.	Vision of the Harmony of Things, Mysteries of the Crucifixion, Beatific Vision
Blumaza	Dispensing and governing the heptarchial doctrine.	Vision of the Machinery of the Universe
Babalel	Who art King of Waters: Mighty and Wonderful in Waters.	Vision of Power
Bnaspol	To whom the Earth with her bowels, and secrets what so ever are delivered.	Vision of Splendour, as seen in the Book of Ezekiel
Bynepor	Whose exalted, especial and glorified Power, resteth only and dependeth the general condition of all things.	Vision of Love
Baligon	Who canst distribute and bestow at pleasure, all and whatsoever can be wrought in aerial actions.	Vision of Beauty Triumphant
Bnapsen	Casting out the power of all wicked spirits, knowing the doings and practices of evil men.	Vision of Sorrow / Vision of Wonder

Table 8. Powers of the Kings

It should be obvious that selecting the proper King or Prince is vitally important to the success of your operation. Like all spirits, the Kings and Princes have particular areas that represent their spheres of influence and must operate within those areas. According to workings performed by my magical group, they possess the powers of the planet to which they are attributed in addition to those delineated in their particular conjurations. The traditional powers shown are from Aleister Crowley's *"Liber 777"* (Column XLV.) and are similar to those found in Agrippa and other Renaissance sources. The Kings are related to traditional mystical visions because they represent knowledge and illumination rather than material action.

The Princes correspond to the magical powers related to the planets, by day rather than by hour. So, for example, even though Bornogo is attributed to the hour of Venus, his powers correspond to the Sun because he is the Prince for Sunday.

Prince	Conjuration Powers	Traditional Powers
Hagonel	To whose Power the Operation of the Earth is subject.	The White Tincture, Clairvoyance, Divination by Dreams.
Bornogo	Altering of the Corruption of Nature into perfection, Knowledge of Metals.	Power of Acquiring Wealth.
Bralges	Who saidst: The Creatures living in thy Dominion are subject to thy own power.	The White Tincture, Clairvoyance, Divination by Dreams.
Befafes	Who art Prince of the Seas. Thy Power is upon the Waters.	Works of Wrath and Vengeance.
Blisdon	Who art Life and Breath in Living Creatures.	Miracles of Healing, Gift of Tongues, Knowledge of Sciences.
Butmono	Unto whom, the Keys of the Mysteries of the Earth are delivered.	Power of Acquiring Political and other Ascendency.
Bagenol	To whose Power the Operation of the Earth is subject.	Love-philtres.
Brorges	Who governs the "gates of death."	Works of Malediction and Death.

Table 9. Powers of the Princes

Physical Manifestations:

In *"Ceremonial Magick and the Power of Evocation"* Joseph Lisiewski is particularly vehement in his argument that for an evocation to succeed the spirit conjured must produce some sort of physical manifestation. While I have never worked with the spirits of the *"Heptameron"* as Lisiewski does, I can say from personal experience that this is not the case with the angels of the *"Heptarchia Mystica"*. The most extreme physical effects I have encountered when working with them are temperature fluctuations in the room and/or over the Holy Table and, when using a candle in the center of the Sigillum Dei Aemeth as a spell focus, unusual behavior of the flame when the angel is present.

Despite this, in terms of accomplishing specific magical objectives the Kings and Princes are very effective whether or not even these physical effects manifest during a given ritual. The determination of a ritual's success or failure should depend on only one factor — whether or not the objective of the operation is achieved. It should not make any difference whether or not you see the spirit, whether or not you hear unexplained sounds, or even whether on not your spell focus explodes as you complete the conjuration. Such things are peripheral phenomena unrelated to the operation at hand, and obsession with them can lead to a profound misunderstanding of the nature of the magical arts.

As mentioned in Chapter 5, Dee and Kelley placed a crystal sphere in the center of the Sigillum and conjured the various angels with whom they worked into it. If you are a skilled scryer or are working with one you may wish to do the same. One scrying method that we are experimenting with in my magical working group is to use a brain machine, a device that synchronizes brainwaves using light and sound. Prior to the scrying session, the scryer runs an alpha/theta brainwave program on the machine for at least ten minutes. *Theta Waves* are the lowest frequency brainwaves that normally occur during waking consciousness, and *Alpha Waves* are the next highest class of frequencies and correspond to relaxed attention. These two classes of waves have been measured as heightened in subjects engaged in meditation, so our working hypothesis was that cultivating them would facilitate scrying. From the testing we have been able to do it appears to work, though if you already are good at scrying and can enter the proper state easily on your own it probably will not make much difference in your results. The machine we use is a Photosonix Nova Pro 100[1] which is one of the most expensive models, but alpha/theta programs are standard for basic meditation and can be found on less expensive machines as well.

Heptarchial Talismans:

The *"Heptarchia Mystica"* includes a series of names and sigils to be drawn onto seven talismans, one for each day of the week, plus an eighth for Carmara and Hagonel. The same talisman is used for the King and for the corresponding Prince. The designs shown here are similar to those published by Geoffrey James in *"The Enochian Magick of Doctor John Dee"*, except that the names of the King and Prince as well as those lining the border of the circle have been rendered into Angelic characters.

One oddity about heptarchial magick is that rather than the talisman being held or somehow drawn onto a scrying mirror, the magician must instead place the talisman on the floor and stand upon it while reciting the conjuration. As far as I have been able to discern this is a unique method that is not found in any of the other grimoires that were available during the Renaissance. The seven talismans must thus be drawn or photocopied large enough to stand upon. Also, in the text of the *"Heptarchia Mystica"* the sigils for the Kings and associated names are shown with English letters, but it is my contention that in order to properly activate the talismans these characters must be transposed into the Angelic. I have not included the English versions here as they are easily found on other works, most notably Joseph Peterson's edition of John Dee's Five Books of Mystery. Peterson also maintains an online copy of the *"Heptarchia Mystica"* at his Esoteric Archives web site that shows the English lettering.[2]

Before presenting the sigils for the Kings and Princes, Caramara showed Dee an image of a flag with a woman on one side, the old flag of England on the other, and the letters B and C. Carmara refered to this image as "the sign of the work." Some sources have misinterpreted the image as some sort of sigil for Carmara, but this is incorrect. To

---

1. More information on the Nova Pro can be found at http://photosonix.com/nova_pro_100.htm.
2. Joseph H. Peterson, ed. Heptarchia Mystica (1997: Retrieved 4/12/2011 from http://www.esotericarchives. com/dee/hm.htm)

my way of thinking the image alludes to one of Dee's key purposes in pursuing magical knowledge — to aid his queen and country. The woman represents Dee's patron, Queen Elizabeth I, the flag signifies the nation of Britain, and the B and C likely allude to the British Crown. Dee was then shown a second image, of the word EL. I believe that this word is an allusion to the sigil for Carmara, which is the same as the sigil for Baligon, an oblong triangle containing that particular name. Dee further notes that Baligon and Carmara are the same entity and appear in the same manner. Likewise, Blumaza also represents an aspect of Carmara. No ring of names is given for Blumaza, though Dee does record a specific sigil. The talisman for Blumaza therefore uses the same outer ring of letters as does the talisman for Carmara, though it is otherwise contructed using Blumaza's unique seal. Finally, Dee gives no seal for Bagenol,[3] but as he is the Prince corresponding to Baligon it follows that he corresponds to Hagonel and therefore has the same seal.

Images of the talismans follow, and those that I use are drawn eight inches in diameter on 8 ½ x 11 inch sheets of paper. I find that this is a good size that allows both feet to touch the image without my having to stand in an awkward position.

---

3. Joseph H. Peterson, ed. Heptarchia Mystica (1997: Retrieved 4/12/2011 from http://www.esotericarchives. com/dee/hm.htm)

Figure 44. Talisman for Carmara and Hagonel

Figure 45. Talisman for Sunday, Bobogel and Bornogo

Figure 46. Talisman for Monday, Blumaza and Bralges

Figure 47. Talisman for Tuesday, Babalel and Befafes

Figure 48. Talisman for Wednesday, Bnaspol and Blisdon

Figure 49. Talisman for Thursday, Bynepor and Butmono

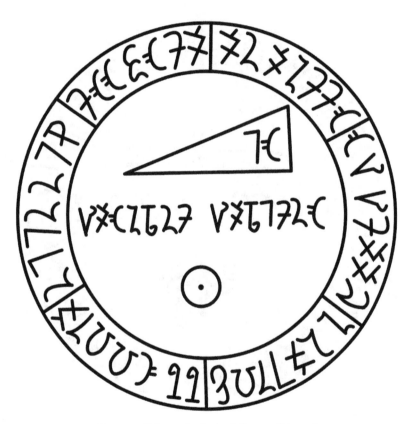

Figure 50. Talisman for Friday, Baligon and Bagenol

Figure 51 Talisman for Saturday, Bnapsen and Brorges

The Kings

All of the Heptarchial Kings are summoned using the same conjuration, with the King's name and office inserted into the conjuration itself. There is a King for each of the seven days of the week, and a different King rules each day. You should only attempt to summon a King on the appropriate day of the week and during the planetary hour that matches the day. Bobogel, for example, the King for Sunday, should be summoned only on that day during the hour of the Sun.

King CARMARA is the one special case. He is the overall ruler of the Heptarchial Angels and may be summoned on any day of the week and during the hour of any planet. However, this same Angel also appears as BLUMAZA, in which guise he is the King for Monday and should be summoned on that day during the hour of the Moon. His powers and abilities remain the same regardless of the name by which he is conjured. The conjurations for CARMARA and BLUMAZA are essentially the same, the only difference being the name of the King.

The offices for each King are reproduced as they appear in the "Heptarchia Mystica", although a small amount of editing was required in order to fit the conjurations together. As with the Keys, each appears on its own page for use with the Heptarchial Ritual Template rather than Dee's format, in which the conjuration was shown once and the magician was expected to insert the office of the King into it. I have also italicized portions of the conjurations that are clearly personal and directly related to Dee's work so that you may omit those particular comments in your own work if you so desire.

In addition to the offices named for each of the Kings they also embody the traditional powers of the seven ancient planets and behave for the most part like planetary intelligences. Their primary function is to know rather than to do. Accomplishing specific tasks is more properly associated with the Princes, whereas the Kings are more appropriate to workings seeking greater knowledge and spiritual illumination related to their particular planetary spheres. Note in the conjuration, however, that when the King is summoned the Prince will also be present, so in a single operation you can summon a King in order to obtain more information about a situation and then charge the corresponding Prince to make some sort of change to that situation based.

King Carmara

Image:

A well-proportioned man dressed in a long purple robe with a triple crown of gold upon his head. He holds a golden measuring rod in his hand divided into three equal parts.

Conjuration:

O puissant and right Noble King CARMARA and by what name est thou art called, or mayst truly and duly be called: Who in the Heptarchical Doctrine, at Blessed Uriel his hand, didst receive the golden rod of government and measuring, and the chain of Dignity and Doctrine: And didst appear first to us, adorned with a Triple Diadem in a long purple robe. Who saidst to me at Mortlake: I minister the strength of God unto thee. Likewise, thou saidst: These Mysteries hath God Lastly, and of his great Mercies, granted unto thee. Thou shalt be glutted, yea filled: yea, thou shalt swell and be puffed up, with the perfect Knowledge of God's Mysteries, in His mercies. And saidst: This Art, is to the further Understanding of all Science, that are past, present, or yet to come. And Immediately, didst say unto me: Kings there are in Nature, with Nature, and above Nature. Thou art Dignified. And saidst, concerning the use of these Tables, This is but the first step: Neither shalt thou practice them in vain: And saidst, thus generally of God's mercies and Graces on me decreed and bestowed. Whatsoever thou shalt speak, do or work, shall be profitable and acceptable. And the end shall be good.

In the Name of the King of Kings, the Lord of Hosts, the Almighty God, Creator of Heaven and Earth, and of all things visible and invisible: O right Noble King CARMARA, Come now and Appear, with thy Prince and his Ministers, and subjects, to my perfect and sensible eye of Judgment: in a goodly and friendly manner, to my comfort and help, for the advancing of the Honor and Glory of our Almighty God by my service. As much as by thy Wisdom and Power, in thy proper Kingly office and Government, I may be holden and enabled unto: Amen.

Come, O right Noble King CARMARA I say, Come, Amen.

Christian:

Gloria Patri, et Filio, et Spiritui Sancto, Sicut erat in principio, et nunc, et semper, et in saecula saeculorum. Amen.

Thelemic:

Gloria Patri et Matri et Filio et Filiae et Spiritui Sancto externo et Spiritui Sancto interno ut erat est erit in saecula Saeculorum sex in uno per nomen Septem in uno Ararita. Amen.

Sunday: King Bobogel (Sun)

Image:

A man with a long beard richly dressed in a black velvet coat, hose with velvet upperstocks overlaid with gold lace, a velvet cap with a black feather in it, and a cape hanging over one shoulder. A purse hangs around his neck and a gilt rapier is at his belt.

Conjuration:

O puissant and right Noble King BOBOGEL and by what name est thou art called, or mayst truly and duly be called: To whose peculiar Government, charge, Disposition, and Kingly office doth appertain the distributing, giving and bestowing of Wisdom and Science. The Teaching of True Philosophy, true understanding of all Learning, grounded upon wisdom: Truth and Excellencies in Nature: and of many other great Mysteries, marvelously available, and necessary to the advancing of the Glory of our God and Creator. And who sayest to me (in respect of these Mysteries attaining) Dee, Dee, Dee, At length, but not too late.

In the Name of the King of Kings, the Lord of Hosts, the Almighty God, Creator of Heaven and Earth, and of all things visible and invisible: O right Noble King BOBOGEL, Come now and Appear, with thy Prince and his Ministers, and subjects, to my perfect and sensible eye of Judgment: in a goodly and friendly manner, to my comfort and help, for the advancing of the Honor and Glory of our Almighty God by my service. As much as by thy Wisdom and Power, in thy proper Kingly office and Government, I may be holden and enabled unto: Amen.

Come, O right Noble King BOBOGEL I say, Come, Amen.

Christian:

Gloria Patri, et Filio, et Spiritui Sancto, Sicut erat in principio, et nunc, et semper, et in saecula saeculorum. Amen.

Thelemic:

Gloria Patri et Matri et Filio et Filiae et Spiritui Sancto externo et Spiritui Sancto interno ut erat est erit in saecula Saeculorum sex in uno per nomen Septem in uno Ararita. Amen.

Monday: King Blumaza (Moon)

Image:

None given in the text, though possibly the same as for Carmara - A well-proportioned man dressed in a long purple robe with a triple crown of gold upon his head. He holds a golden measuring rod in his hand divided into three equal parts.

Conjuration:

O puissant and right Noble King BLUMAZA and by what name est thou art called, or mayst truly and duly be called: Who in the Heptarchical Doctrine, at Blessed Uriel his hand, didst receive the golden rod of government and measuring, and the chain of Dignity and Doctrine: And didst appear first to us, adorned with a Triple Diadem in a long purple robe. Who saidst to me at Mortlake: I minister the strength of God unto thee. Likewise, thou saidst: These Mysteries hath God Lastly, and of his great Mercies, granted unto thee. Thou shalt be glutted, yea filled: yea, thou shalt swell and be puffed up, with the perfect Knowledge of God's Mysteries, in His mercies. And saidst: This Art, is to the further Understanding of all Science, that are past, present, or yet to come. And Immediately, didst say unto me: Kings there are in Nature, with Nature, and above Nature. Thou art Dignified. And saidst, concerning the use of these Tables, This is but the first step: Neither shalt thou practice them in vain: And saidst, thus generally of God's mercies and Graces on me decreed and bestowed. Whatsoever thou shalt speak, do or work, shall be profitable and acceptable. And the end shall be good.

In the Name of the King of Kings, the Lord of Hosts, the Almighty God, Creator of Heaven and Earth, and of all things visible and invisible: O right Noble King BLUMAZA, Come now and Appear, with thy Prince and his Ministers, and subjects, to my perfect and sensible eye of Judgment: in a goodly and friendly manner, to my comfort and help, for the advancing of the Honor and Glory of our Almighty God by my service. As much as by thy Wisdom and Power, in thy proper Kingly office and Government, I may be holden and enabled unto: Amen.

Come, O right Noble King BLUMAZA I say, Come, Amen.

Christian:

Gloria Patri, et Filio, et Spiritui Sancto, Sicut erat in principio, et nunc, et semper, et in saecula saeculorum. Amen.

Thelemic:

Gloria Patri et Matri et Filio et Filiae et Spiritui Sancto externo et Spiritui Sancto interno ut erat est erit in saecula Saeculorum sex in uno per nomen Septem in uno Ararita. Amen.

Tuesday: King Babalel (Mars)

Image:

A man with a crown of gold on his head dressed in a long whitish robe. His left sleeve is bright white and his right sleeve is black. He seems to stand upon water, and his name is written across his forehead.

Conjuration:

O puissant and right Noble King BABALEL and by what name est thou art called, or mayst truly and duly be called: Who art King of Waters: Mighty and Wonderful in Waters, Whose power is in the bowels of the Waters. Whose Royal person with thy Nobel Prince BEFAFES and his 42 Ministers the Triple Crowned King CARMARA bade me use to the glory praise and honor of him, which created you all to the Laud and praise of his majesty.

In the Name of the King of Kings, the Lord of Hosts, the Almighty God, Creator of Heaven and Earth, and of all things visible and invisible: O right Noble King BABALEL, Come now and Appear, with thy

Prince and his Ministers, and subjects, to my perfect and sensible eye of Judgment: in a goodly and friendly manner, to my comfort and help, for the advancing of the Honor and Glory of our Almighty God by my service. As much as by thy Wisdom and Power, in thy proper Kingly office and Government, I may be holden and enabled unto: Amen.

Come, O right Noble King BABALEL I say, Come, Amen.

Christian:

Gloria Patri, et Filio, et Spiritui Sancto, Sicut erat in principio, et nunc, et semper, et in saecula saeculorum. Amen.

Thelemic:

Gloria Patri et Matri et Filio et Filiae et Spiritui Sancto externo et Spiritui Sancto interno ut erat est erit in saecula Saeculorum sex in uno per nomen Septem in uno Ararita. Amen.

Wednesday: King Bnaspol (Mercury)

Image:

A man with a crown on his head dressed in a red robe.

Conjuration:

O puissant and right Noble King BNASPOL and by what name est thou art called, or mayst truly and duly be called: To whom the Earth with her bowels, and secrets what so ever are delivered: and hast said to me: here to fore What thou Art. There I may know. Thou art great but (as Thou, truly didst confess). He in whom Thou art is greater than thou.

In the Name of the King of Kings, the Lord of Hosts, the Almighty God, Creator of Heaven and Earth, and of all things visible and invisible: O right Noble King BNASPOL, Come now and Appear, with thy Prince and his Ministers, and subjects, to my perfect and sensible eye of Judgment: in a goodly and friendly manner, to my comfort and help, for the advancing of the Honor and Glory of our Almighty God by my service. As much as by thy Wisdom and Power, in thy proper Kingly office and Government, I may be holden and enabled unto: Amen.

Come, O right Noble King BNASPOL I say, Come, Amen.

Christian:

Gloria Patri, et Filio, et Spiritui Sancto, Sicut erat in principio, et nunc, et semper, et in saecula saeculorum. Amen.

Thelemic:

Gloria Patri et Matri et Filio et Filiae et Spiritui Sancto externo et Spiritui Sancto interno ut erat est erit in saecula Saeculorum sex in uno per nomen Septem in uno Ararita. Amen.

Thursday: King Bynepor (Jupiter)

Image:

A man dressed and outfitted as a traditional king, wearing a golden crown.

Conjuration:

O puissant and right Noble King BYNEPOR and by what name est thou art called, or mayst truly and duly be called: To whose peculiar Government, charge, Disposition, and Kingly office doth appertain thee upon the distribution and participation of whose exalted, especial and glorified Power, resteth only and dependeth the general condition of all things. Whose sanctification, glory and renown, although it had beginning, yet can it not neither shall have ending. He that measureth said, and thou was the end of his workmanship. Thou are like him and of him: yet not as partaking or adherent, but different in one degree. Whom he came, thou wast magnified by his coming and art Sanctified, World without End.

Vita Suprema.

Vita Superior.

Vita Infina tuis sunt mensurata mambus.

Not withstanding thou art not of thyself: neither is thy power thine own: Magnified be his name, Thou art in all: And all hath some being by thee: Yet thy Power is Nothing, in respect of his power, which hath sent thee. Thou beginnest new Worlds, new people, New Kings, and New Knowledge of a New Government. And hast said to me: Thou shalt work marvelous, Marvelously by my workmanship in the Highest.

In the Name of the King of Kings, the Lord of Hosts, the Almighty God, Creator of Heaven and Earth, and of all things visible and invisible: O right Noble King BYNEPOR, Come now and Appear, with thy Prince and his Ministers, and subjects, to my perfect and sensible eye of Judgment: in a goodly and friendly manner, to my comfort and help, for the advancing of the Honor and Glory of our Almighty God by my service. As much as by thy Wisdom and Power, in thy proper Kingly office and Government, I may be holden and enabled unto: Amen.

Come, O right Noble King BYNEPOR I say, Come, Amen.

Christian:

Gloria Patri, et Filio, et Spiritui Sancto, Sicut erat in principio, et nunc, et semper, et in saecula saeculorum. Amen.

Thelemic:

Gloria Patri et Matri et Filio et Filiae et Spiritui Sancto externo et Spiritui Sancto interno ut erat est erit in saecula Saeculorum sex in uno per nomen Septem in uno Ararita. Amen.

Friday: King Baligon (Venus)

Image:

A well-proportioned man dressed in a long purple robe with a triple crown of gold upon his head. He holds a golden measuring rod in his hand divided into three equal parts.

Conjuration:

O puissant and right Noble King BALIGON and by what name est thou art called, or mayst truly and duly be called: Who canst distribute and bestow at pleasure, all and whatsoever can be wrought in aerial actions. Who hast the government of thy self perfectly, as a Mystery known only unto thy self. Who didst advertise me of this stone, and Holy Receptacle: both needful to be had: and also didst direct me to the taking of it up: being presently and in a few minutes of time, brought to my sight (from the Secret of the Depth, where it was hid, in the uttermost part of the Roman possession) Which stone, Thou, warnedst me, that no mortal hand but mine own shall touch: and saidst unto me: Thou shall prevail with it, with Kings, and with all the Creatures of the

World. Whose Beauty (in virtue) shall be more worth, that the Kingdoms of the Earth. For the purposes here rehearsed: and other: partly, now to be exercised and enjoyed: and partly hereafter more abundantly (as the Lord God of Hosts shall Dispose), And also because thou thy self art Governor of the 42 thy Mighty Faithful, and Obedient Ministers.

In the Name of the King of Kings, the Lord of Hosts, the Almighty God, Creator of Heaven and Earth, and of all things visible and invisible: O right Noble King BALIGON, Come now and Appear, with thy Prince and his Ministers, and subjects, to my perfect and sensible eye of Judgment: in a goodly and friendly manner, to my comfort and help, for the advancing of the Honor and Glory of our Almighty God by my service. As much as by thy Wisdom and Power, in thy proper Kingly office and Government, I may be holden and enabled unto: Amen.

Come, O right Noble King BALIGON I say, Come, Amen.

Christian:

Gloria Patri, et Filio, et Spiritui Sancto, Sicut erat in principio, et nunc, et semper, et in saecula saeculorum. Amen.

Thelemic:

Gloria Patri et Matri et Filio et Filiae et Spiritui Sancto externo et Spiritui Sancto interno ut erat est erit in saecula Saeculorum sex in uno per nomen Septem in uno Ararita. Amen.

Saturday: King Bnapsen (Saturn)

Image:

A man dressed and outfitted as a traditional king, wearing a golden crown.

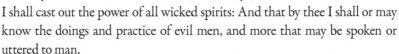

Conjuration:

O puissant and right Noble King BNAPSEN and by what name est thou art called, or mayst truly and duly be called: Who hast said to me that by thee I shall cast out the power of all wicked spirits: And that by thee I shall or may know the doings and practice of evil men, and more that may be spoken or uttered to man.

In the Name of the King of Kings, the Lord of Hosts, the Almighty God, Creator of Heaven and Earth, and of all things visible and invisible:

O right Noble King BNAPSEN, Come now and Appear, with thy Prince and his Ministers, and subjects, to my perfect and sensible eye of Judgment: in a goodly and friendly manner, to my comfort and help, for the advancing of the Honor and Glory of our Almighty God by my service. As much as by thy Wisdom and Power, in thy proper Kingly office and Government, I may be holden and enabled unto: Amen.

Come, O right Noble King BNAPSEN I say, Come, Amen.

Christian:

Gloria Patri, et Filio, et Spiritui Sancto, Sicut erat in principio, et nunc, et semper, et in saecula saeculorum. Amen.

Thelemic:

Gloria Patri et Matri et Filio et Filiae et Spiritui Sancto externo et Spiritui Sancto interno ut erat est erit in saecula Saeculorum sex in uno per nomen Septem in uno Ararita. Amen.

The Princes

All of the Princes are summoned using the same invocation, with the Prince's name and office inserted into the invocation itself. There is a Prince for each of the seven days of the week, each corresponding to a particular King. The planetary hours attributed to the Princes are shown next to their names and they should be conjured on the proper day during the designated hour. So the Prince for Sunday (the Sun) should be summoned during the hour of Venus, that for Monday (the Moon) during the hour of Saturn, that for Tuesday (Mars) during the hour of the Sun, and so on as explained in Chapter 9.

When tuning the space with ceremonial forms you will want to use the Greater Ritual of the Hexagram for the planet hour attributed to the Prince, not the planet attributed to the day. This may seem somewhat odd when, for example, performing a ritual attributed to Jupiter on a Thursday but then using the Greater Hexagram of Mars to tune the space. The rationale, however, is that the Prince represents the flow of Mezla or magical manifestation emanating from the sphere of Jupiter and beginning its transition into the material world by shifting into the sphere of Mars.

Prince HAGONEL is the Prince corresponding to CARMARA, and as a result may be called by that name on any day of the week. However, like

CARMARA he also appears under an alternate name — as BAGENOL he is the Prince associated with Friday and the hour of Mercury. His powers are the same regardless of the name used to summon him.

Prince Hagonel

Image:

A man dressed in a short red robe with a golden circlet on his head.

Conjuration:

O noble Prince HAGONEL and by what Name else ever thou art called, or mayst truly, and duly be called: To whose commandment the sons of men and their sons are subject: and are thy servants To whose Power the Operation of the Earth is subject. Who art the First of the Twelve: and whose seal is called Barces and this it is: At whose commandment, are the Kings, Noble men, and Princes of Nature. Who art Primus et Quartus Hagonel. Who by the Seven of the 7 (which are the Sons of Sempiternitie) dost work marvels amongst the people of the Earth: and hath said to me, that I also By the same thy Servant, should work marvels. O Noble Hagonel, who Art Minister to the Triple crowned King — CARMARA: And notwithstanding art Prince over these 42 Angels, whose Names and characters are here presented.

In the Name of the Almighty God, the King of Kings, And for his honor and Glory to be advanced by my faithful Service. I require thee, O Noble Prince HAGONEL to come presently, and to show thy self to my perfect and sensible eye of Judgement, with thy Ministers, servants and subjects, to my comfort and help, in wisdom and power according to the property of thy Noble Office:

Come, O Noble Prince HAGONEL I say Come, Amen.

Christian:

Pater noster, qui es in caelis, sanctificetur nomen tuum. Adveniat regnum tuum. Fiat voluntas tua, sicut in caelo et in terra. Panem nostrum quotidianum da nobis hodie, et dimitte nobis debita nostra sicut et nos dimittimus debitoribus nostris. Et ne nos inducas in tentationem, sed libera nos a malo. Amen.

Thelemic:

Now I begin to pray, thou child, holy thy name and undefiled. Thy reign is come, thy will is done, here is the bread, here is the blood, bring me through midnight to the Sun. Save me from evil and from good, that thy one crown of all the ten even now and here be mine. Amen.

Sunday: Prince Bornogo (Venus)

Image:

A man in a long red robe with a golden circlet on his head.

Conjuration:

O noble Prince BORNOGO and by what Name else ever thou art called, or mayst truly, and duly be called: To whose peculiar Government, Charge and Disposition, Office and Princely Dignity doth appertain the Altering of the Corruption of Nature into perfection: The Knowledge of Metals. And generally the Princely Ministering to the right Noble and Mighty King BOBOGEL, in his government: Of Distributing, giving and bestowing of Wisdom, Science, True Philosophy and true understanding of all learning grounded upon wisdom and of other very many his peculiar Royal Properties. And who sayeth to me: What thou desireth in me shall be fulfilled.

In the Name of the Almighty God, the King of Kings, And for his honor and Glory to be advanced by my faithful Service. I require thee, O Noble Prince BORNOGO to come presently, and to show thy self to my perfect and sensible eye of Judgement, with thy Ministers, servants and subjects, to my comfort and help, in wisdom and power according to the property of thy Noble Office:

Come, O Noble Prince BORNOGO I say Come, Amen.

Christian:

Pater noster, qui es in caelis, sanctificetur nomen tuum. Adveniat regnum tuum. Fiat voluntas tua, sicut in caelo et in terra. Panem nostrum quotidianum da nobis hodie, et dimitte nobis debita nostra sicut et nos dimittimus debitoribus nostris. Et ne nos inducas in tentationem, sed libera nos a malo. Amen.

Thelemic:

Now I begin to pray, thou child, holy thy name and undefiled. Thy reign is come, thy will is done, here is the bread, here is the blood, bring me through midnight to the Sun. Save me from evil and from good, that thy one crown of all the ten even now and here be mine. Amen.

Monday: Prince Bralges (Saturn)

Image:

A man in a long red robe with a golden circlet on his head.

Conjuration:

O noble Prince BRALGES and by what Name else ever thou art called, or mayst truly, and duly be called: Who saidst: The Creatures living in thy Dominion are subject to thy own power. Whose subjects are Invisible: And which (to my Seer) appeared like little smokes without any form. Whose seal of government is this: Who saidst: Behold I am come, I will teach the Name without numbers. The Creatures Subject unto me shall be known unto you.

In the Name of the Almighty God, the King of Kings, And for his honor and Glory to be advanced by my faithful Service. I require thee, O Noble Prince BRALGES to come presently, and to show thy self to my perfect and sensible eye of Judgement, with thy Ministers, servants and subjects, to my comfort and help, in wisdom and power according to the property of thy Noble Office:

Come, O Noble Prince BRALGES I say Come, Amen.

Christian:

Pater noster, qui es in caelis, sanctificetur nomen tuum. Adveniat regnum tuum. Fiat voluntas tua, sicut in caelo et in terra. Panem nostrum quotidianum da nobis hodie, et dimitte nobis debita nostra sicut et nos dimittimus debitoribus nostris. Et ne nos inducas in tentationem, sed libera nos a malo. Amen.

Thelemic:

Now I begin to pray, thou child, holy thy name and undefiled. Thy reign is come, thy will is done, here is the bread, here is the blood, bring me through midnight to the Sun. Save me from evil and from good, that thy one crown of all the ten even now and here be mine. Amen.

Tuesday: Prince Befafes (Sun)

Image:

A man in a long red robe with a circlet on his head. He wears a golden girdle with his name written on it, his chest appears lean, and he seems to have feathers under his robe.

Conjuration:

O noble Prince BEFAFES and by what Name else ever thou art called, or mayst truly, and duly be called: Who art Prince of the Seas. Thy Power is upon the Waters. Thou drownst Pharaoh and hast destroyed the wicked. Thy Name was known to Moses. Thou livedst in Israel: who hast measured the waters, who wast with King Solomon, and also long after that with Scotus: but not known to him by thy true Name: for he called thee Maris. And since, thou wast with none: Except, when thou preserved me (though the mercy of God), from the power of the wicked: and wast with me in extremity. Thou wast with me thoroughly.[4] Who of the Egyptians, hath been called OBELISON in respect of thy pleasant deliverance. And by that Name to me known: and of me noted in record, to be Noble and courteous OBELISON. Whose Noble Ministers 42 are of very great power, dignity, and Authority. As some in the measuring of the motions of the Waters, and saltiness of the Seas, in giving good success in battles reducing ships, and all manner of vessels that float upon the Seas. To some all the fishes and Monsters of the Seas, yea, all that liveth therein are well known: And generally are the Distributors of God's Judgements upon the Waters that cover the Earth. Others do beautify Nature in her composition. The rest are distributors and Deliverers of the Therefore and unknown substances of the Seas. Thou O Noble Prince BEFAFES hadst me use in the Name of God.

In the Name of the Almighty God, the King of Kings, And for his honor and Glory to be advanced by my faithful Service. I require thee, O Noble Prince

---

4. This particular personal note of Dee's combined with the power of "giving good success in battles reducing ships" suggests to some magicians that Dee may have summoned this Prince to help the English defeat the Spanish Armada in 1588. If this is ever found to be the case, it would refute those authors who claimed that Dee never actually made use of the magical system that he and Kelley developed.

BEFAFES to come presently, and to show thy self to my perfect and sensible eye of Judgement, with thy Ministers, servants and subjects, to my comfort and help, in wisdom and power according to the property of thy Noble Office:

Come, O Noble Prince BEFAFES I say Come, Amen.

Christian:

Pater noster, qui es in caelis, sanctificetur nomen tuum. Adveniat regnum tuum. Fiat voluntas tua, sicut in caelo et in terra. Panem nostrum quotidianum da nobis hodie, et dimitte nobis debita nostra sicut et nos dimittimus debitoribus nostris. Et ne nos inducas in tentationem, sed libera nos a malo. Amen.

Thelemic:

Now I begin to pray, thou child, holy thy name and undefiled. Thy reign is come, thy will is done, here is the bread, here is the blood, bring me through midnight to the Sun. Save me from evil and from good, that thy one crown of all the ten even now and here be mine. Amen.

Wednesday: Prince Blisdon (Jupiter)

Image:

A man dressed in a robe of many colors with a golden circlet on his head.

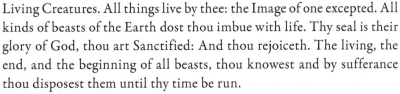

Conjuration:

O noble Prince BLISDON and by what Name else ever thou art called, or mayst truly, and duly be called: Who art Life and breath in Living Creatures. All things live by thee: the Image of one excepted. All kinds of beasts of the Earth dost thou imbue with life. Thy seal is their glory of God, thou art Sanctified: And thou rejoiceth. The living, the end, and the beginning of all beasts, thou knowest and by sufferance thou disposest them until thy time be run.

In the Name of the Almighty God, the King of Kings, And for his honor and Glory to be advanced by my faithful Service. I require thee, O Noble Prince BLISDON to come presently, and to show thy self to my perfect and sensible eye of Judgement, with thy Ministers, servants and subjects, to my comfort and help, in wisdom and power according to the property of thy Noble Office:

Come, O Noble Prince BLISDON I say Come, Amen.

Christian:

Pater noster, qui es in caelis, sanctificetur nomen tuum. Adveniat regnum tuum. Fiat voluntas tua, sicut in caelo et in terra. Panem nostrum quotidianum da nobis hodie, et dimitte nobis debita nostra sicut et nos dimittimus debitoribus nostris. Et ne nos inducas in tentationem, sed libera nos a malo. Amen.

Thelemic:

Now I begin to pray, thou child, holy thy name and undefiled. Thy reign is come, thy will is done, here is the bread, here is the blood, bring me through midnight to the Sun. Save me from evil and from good, that thy one crown of all the ten even now and here be mine. Amen.

Thursday: Prince Butmono (Mars)

Image:

A man dressed in a long red robe with a golden circlet on his head.

Conjuration:

O noble Prince BUTMONO and by what Name else ever thou art called, or mayst truly, and duly be called: Unto whom, the Keys of the  Mysteries of the Earth are delivered. Whose 42 ministers are Angels, that govern under thee. All which thy Mighty King BYNEPOR bade me use and affirmed that they are, and shall be at my commandment.

In the Name of the Almighty God, the King of Kings, And for his honor and Glory to be advanced by my faithful Service. I require thee, O Noble Prince BLISDON to come presently, and to show thy self to my perfect and sensible eye of Judgement, with thy Ministers, servants and subjects, to my comfort and help, in wisdom and power according to the property of thy Noble Office:

Come, O Noble Prince BLISDON I say Come, Amen.

Christian:

Pater noster, qui es in caelis, sanctificetur nomen tuum. Adveniat regnum tuum. Fiat voluntas tua, sicut in caelo et in terra. Panem nostrum quotidianum da nobis hodie, et dimitte nobis debita nostra sicut et nos dimittimus debitoribus nostris. Et ne nos inducas in tentationem, sed libera nos a malo. Amen.

Thelemic:

Now I begin to pray, thou child, holy thy name and undefiled. Thy reign is come, thy will is done, here is the bread, here is the blood, bring me through midnight to the Sun. Save me from evil and from good, that thy one crown of all the ten even now and here be mine. Amen.

Friday: Prince Bagenol (Moon)

Image:

None given in the text, but possibly the same as for Hagonel — a man dressed in a short red robe with a golden circlet on his head.

Conjuration:

O noble Prince BAGENOL and by what Name else ever thou art called, or mayst truly, and duly be called: To whose commandment the sons of men and their sons are subject: and are thy servants To whose Power the Operation of the Earth is subject. Who art the First of the Twelve: and whose seal is called Barces and this it is: At whose commandment, are the Kings, Noble men, and Princes of Nature. Who art Primus et Quartus Hagonel. Who by the Seven of the 7 (which are the Sons of Sempiternitie) dost work marvels amongst the people of the Earth: and hath said to me, that I also By the same thy Servant, should work marvels. O Noble BAGENOL, who Art Minister to the Triple crowned King — BALIGON: And notwithstanding art Prince over these 42 Angels, whose Names and characters are here presented.

In the Name of the Almighty God, the King of Kings, And for his honor and Glory to be advanced by my faithful Service. I require thee, O Noble Prince BAGENOL to come presently, and to show thy self to my perfect and sensible eye of Judgement, with thy Ministers, servants and subjects, to my comfort and help, in wisdom and power according to the property of thy Noble Office:

Come, O Noble Prince BAGENOL I say Come, Amen.

Christian:

Pater noster, qui es in caelis, sanctificetur nomen tuum. Adveniat regnum tuum. Fiat voluntas tua, sicut in caelo et in terra. Panem nostrum quotidianum da nobis hodie, et dimitte nobis debita nostra sicut et nos dimittimus debitoribus nostris. Et ne nos inducas in tentationem, sed libera nos a malo. Amen.

Thelemic:

Now I begin to pray, thou child, holy thy name and undefiled. Thy reign is come, thy will is done, here is the bread, here is the blood, bring me through midnight to the Sun. Save me from evil and from good, that thy one crown of all the ten even now and here be mine. Amen.

Saturday: Prince Brorges (Mercury)

Image:

A man dressed in a long red robe with a golden circlet on his head. Terrible flames blaze from under his clothing in which his name can be seen, tossed to and fro.

Conjuration:

O noble Prince BRORGES and by what Name else ever thou art called, or mayst truly, and duly be called: Who, being the Prince: chief minister and governor under the right Puissant King BNAPSEN didst (to my Seer) appear in a most terrible manner with fire flaming streams, and saidst: Noui Ianaum Mortis. Et per cussit Gloria Dei, Impiorum parietes.

In the Name of the Almighty God, the King of Kings, And for his honor and Glory to be advanced by my faithful Service. I require thee, O Noble Prince BRORGES to come presently, and to show thy self to my perfect and sensible eye of Judgement, with thy Ministers, servants and subjects, to my comfort and help, in wisdom and power according to the property of thy Noble Office:

Come, O Noble Prince BRORGES I say Come, Amen.

Christian:

Pater noster, qui es in caelis, sanctificetur nomen tuum. Adveniat regnum tuum. Fiat voluntas tua, sicut in caelo et in terra. Panem nostrum quotidianum da nobis hodie, et dimitte nobis debita nostra sicut et nos dimittimus debitoribus nostris. Et ne nos inducas in tentationem, sed libera nos a malo. Amen.

Thelemic:

Now I begin to pray, thou child, holy thy name and undefiled. Thy reign is come, thy will is done, here is the bread, here is the blood, bring me through midnight to the Sun. Save me from evil and from good, that thy one crown of all the ten even now and here be mine. Amen.

Chapter 12
The Charge

The Charge to the spirit is your statement of intent that communicates the exact outcome you want your ritual to produce. Because rituals can be performed for just about any purpose you will need to write the Charge yourself for any ritual that you perform, and there are several factors that you need to keep in mind when doing so.

In order to understand these factors and how they work it is necessary to have some understanding of what spirits are and how they work. Aristotle wrote that the universe consists of both Matter and Form. Matter refers to the subatomic particles of which substances are composed and Form refers to how those particles are arranged. At the quantum level, the behavior of every particle is governed by fields of probability waves that are described in physics by what is called the Schroedinger function. There is some debate among quantum physicists as to whether subatomic particles occupy any particular point in space or simply exist as nonlocal probability waves prior to their interaction with some sort of measuring device.

It may be that at the quantum level Matter and Form collapse into each other, or perhaps they remain distinct in some way that we currently lack the proper tools to measure. In either case, the important thing to understand about spirits such as the angels of the mystical heptarchy is that they are beings of pure Form rather than Matter, just like the consciousness of every individual magician, and as beings of Form they are capable of interacting directly with the probability waves of any particular region of space. Those probability waves then influence the likelihood of particular outcomes when the particles within the region subject to this influence manifest as material objects.

This influence is called a **Probability Shift** and is the basic mechanism by which all practical magick works. Human consciousness consists of Form just as that of a spirit does, and with the right combination of training and aptitude a person can learn to use his or her consciousness to make such a probability shift. Even untrained individuals have been found to have the ability to do this to a very small degree according to a series of experiments conducted by the Princeton Engineering Anomalies Reasearch (PEAR) laboratory in which individuals attempted to influence the behavior of quantum diodes, simple random number generators based on the Schroedinger functions of particular radioactive materials. The influence found was tiny, about .01 percent for most individuals,[1] but because of the enormous numbers of computerized trials conducted the result nonetheless proved highly statistically significant.

In order to become an effective practical magician it is usually necessary to have a higher degree of natural aptitude in this area than what is found in the general population. PEAR identified one subject whose baseline ability with the quantum diodes was about .05 percent, five times higher than that of the other test subjects observed.[2] Among all the subjects tested, this individual was probably the only one who was talented enough to get really good results from magical training. In my experience, the ratio of such individuals is somewhere between one person in thirty and one person in fifty depending on the overall population surveyed. Training takes time and effort, but if you possess the necessary aptitude it is well worth it. According to

1. John McCrone, Psychic Powers: What are the Odds? (The New Scientist, November 1994), 34-38.
2. Ibid.

my experimentation over many years, a powerful magician can produce probability shifts of 100 to 1 or more, which can result in some quite impressive ritual successes.

Working with spirits allows magicians to increase these probability shifts even further. As spirits are beings of Form, they require no training in order to interact with their native environment of probability waves. If we declare a variable M as the probability shift that the magician can produce and a second variable S as the probability shift that a particular spirit can produce, the result of the magician conjuring the spirit should be a shift of M + S. So if the magician has trained to the point where his or her consciousness can produce a 20 to 1 shift but needs a 100 to 1 shift for a particular ritual to succeed, the solution is to summon a spirit that can produce a shift of at least 80 to 1. 20 plus 80 yields 100, which should in this case result in a successful outcome. The spirits of the mystical heptarchy seem to have S ratings of at least 100 according to my own probability tests, so they are capable of accomplishing much even when conjured by beginning magicians.

A common question regarding spirits is how they can possibly have any sort of independent existence if multiple magicians can summon the same spirit at the same time. Some have contended that this demonstrates spirits are simply psychological projections that originate in the mind of each magician, but the reality is more complex than this simple psychological model. Spirits are beings of Form, and are thus non-local entities. They exist within the field of probability functions that underlie material reality rather than occupying a particular place and time. In practice, conjuring a spirit is more like tuning your mind to a particular radio frequency than inviting a friend over for coffee. Like a radio signal the spirit can in effect be in many places at once, and it is from the connection between the mind of the magician and the consciouness of the spirit that magical probability shifts arise.

The function of the conjurations and ritual procedures is to establish such a connection in as clear a manner as possible. Once this is done, the Charge can be delivered to the spirit. It is necessary to communicate this Charge as clearly and succinctly as possible. In effect, you need to think like a lawyer. You want to make sure that all your bases are covered so that the spirits cannot misinterpret your commands or twist their meaning. Some of the old grimoires explain that this is necessary because the spirits will always try to mislead the magician out of animosity, but the truth is a lot more pedestrian: spirits are simply literal-minded and magick always seeks the path of least resistance. I have never come across a heptarchial spirit that was hostile to me but I have experienced a number of cases when I got what I asked for rather than what I wanted, especially back when I was starting out and did not understand how to construct a proper Charge.

For example, let's say that you cast a spell asking for a car. Which of these results is more likely – that a stranger on the street will walk up to you and hand over his vehicle, or that you might happen to find a toy car left in your yard by a neighbor's child? Furthermore, even if you encounter the former situation, what do you think the odds are that you will get to keep the car? Generally speaking, the only car that a random stranger is going to give to you is one that is stolen or worse. So you can't just say to the spirits "I command you to bring me a car." What will happen is the most likely outcome, in which the car is either a toy or a stolen vehicle that you have to return soon after receiving it. You need to specify that the car be drivable, that it will serve the function for which you intend to use it, and that you will be able to keep it for as long as you need it.

By the way, do you think it's impossible to summon a car using magick? Not true! Lon Milo DuQuette writes about doing exactly that in *"My Life With The Spirits"*, and not only that, it took the spirit a mere twenty minutes, the car was drivable, and he got to keep it. The Charge in that case was not "bring me a car" but something to the effect of "bring me something that will help me turn my life around in the next twenty minutes." As he had no car with which to look for work and lived in California where a vehicle is pretty much a necessity, a toy car could never have fit the bill and only a real one would have sufficed. The car was a gift from a friend and was in bad enough shape that it was probably not worth selling but it ran for some time, allowing him to find a decent job and commute to it until he could afford to buy a better vehicle.[3]

One of the advantages of working with the heptarchial Kings and Princes is that they tend to be fairly intelligent as spirits go and have

---

3. Lon Milo DuQuette, My Life with the Spirits (York Beach, ME: Red Wheel / Weiser, 1999), 102-108.

some ability to divine your intent in addition to the exact meaning of your charge. In the Enochian system the length of a spirit's name will tell you roughly how "smart" they are. More letters means more intelligence, and more intelligence gives you a little more leeway in terms of the exactness of your charge. For example, the Great Table includes a class of malevolent spirits that Dee called the cacodemons. These spirits have three-letter names and can be powerful when used properly but are also particularly stupid in practice. They will do exactly as they are told — no more, no less. Angels such as the heptarchial Kings and Princes who have seven-letter names are much more intelligent and can think for themselves to a much greater degree. Nevertheless, a well-constructed charge will still help them focus on exactly what you want them to do and prevent any misunderstandings.

A charge consists of two parts, a series of ***Injuctions*** and a series of ***Limitations***. The first explains what you want the spirit to do and the second explains what you do not want the spirit to do. As a simple example, let's say that you need money and summon a spirit to bring you five thousand dollars. There are number of ways in which such a demand could manifest, and some of them are things that you usually do not want. A death in the family could result in an inheritance. You or one of your children could be injured in a traffic accident and receive a settlement that covers little more than your medical bills. You could have a house fire that results in a settlement from your homeowner's insurance of the requested amount. Your car could be totaled in an accident, again bringing you the desired sum but requiring you to spend it on a new vehicle. And the list goes on. So a properly constructed charge in this case would be something to the effect of this:

> I hereby command that you bring me the sum of five thousand dollars within one month (injuction), without causing harm or damage to myself, my loved ones, or my property (limitation).

Every injuction should be given an amount of time in which to work. This is necessary because while the magical probability shift results from the connection between you and a particular spirit, that channel can only produce a total probability shift of a particular magnitude. Think of it as a computer running programs. It can multitask, but as it does the processing power devoted to each program decreases. Without time limits on spells you can sometimes lose track of something that you have "running" and as a result the probability shift you can produce working with a particular spirit will be decreased. If the spell is given a time limit it will either terminate when its objective is achieved or when the time limit runs out.

A good way to work around the multitasking problem is to conjure different spirits for different tasks. Your personal magical power will still be divided among the spells that you have running, but the power of each spirit will not be if each is performing a single separate task. Going back to our equation, if a magician with M of 20 has two spells running involving different spirits, each with S of 100, the result will be (M/2) + S, yielding a probability shift of 110 to 1 for each spell. As you can see, especially with multiple spells, working with spirits is quite advantageous for any magician and can result in much greater effective power than even the best magician could achieve using only his or her mind and aptitudes. This is why practically all magical traditions involve working with spirits — because it really does produce better results.

In order to get the best possible results you should not specify the means by which your objective should be accomplished and rely only on the limitations contained as the second part of your charge to exclude specific undesirable outcomes. This is because you want to make sure that the objective of the spell is not accomplished in some way that undermines the result, but at the same time you want to keep as many paths open as possible for the effect to manifest. Often the best way that something can manifest in your life is not obvious, so it is better to focus on the end result in constructing your magical intent.

As in most medieval grimoires, the angels of the *Heptarchia Mystica* follow a particular spiritual hierarchy.

- King Carmara rules over all the Kings.
- King Carmara rules over Prince Hagonel.
- Prince Hagonel rules over all the Princes.
- Each King rules over the Prince of the corresponding day.

While the *Heptarchia Mystica* is unusual among grimoires in that this hierarchy is not reflected in the conjurations themselves, it can prove useful when constructing particular charges. If the day is such that you cannot summon the King or Prince that corresponds to the goal of your magical operation, you can instead summon Carmara or Hagonel and instruct them to command the King or Prince that you really want to summon to accomplish the desired task.

For example, let's say that you need to perform a practical operation attributed to Earth but the only day on which you can do the ritual is a Sunday. The Prince you really want to conjure is Butmono, to whom "the Keys of the Earth" are delivered, who can only be conjured on a Thursday. In order to accomplish your objective you could conjure and instruct Hagonel to order Butmono to accomplish your goal. The one limitation of this method is that your goal will not be set in motion until the next Thursday rolls around, since Butmono can only initiate actions on the appropriate day.

You will always want to make a note of your precise charge in your magical journal for every operation you perform. If a spell seems to have failed, you can then look back over your charge and see if anything happened that fit the literal instructions you gave but not your true intent. Similarly, if a spell seems particularly effective you will want to keep track of the charge so that you can use it as a model or basis for subsequent operations.

Chapter 13
Closing the Temple

Once you have summoned the proper angel and delivered your charge, the final step is to send the angel forth to accomplish your magical objective and close the temple. In traditional grimoire evocations, spirits are dismissed using a License to Depart, but no such license is present in the Dee material. Based on his reading of the Dee diaries, Robert Turner speculates that Heptarchial evocations were concluded with prayers of thanksgiving offered to the angels, but no record of what these prayers were has survived and Dee did not include them in the text of the *Heptarchia Mystica*.

I particularly like this License that my magical working group has been using for quite a few years. The original version was intended to work as a sort of "bookend" to the Fundamental Obeisance used as the preliminary invocation for opening the Great Table, but the version shown here has been modified for use with the Oration to God for conjurations of the heptarchial Kings and Princes. The references to True Will are explicitly Thelemic and are shown in italics because a Christian magician may want to omit them, though Saint Augustine's comment that one should "love, and do what thou wilt"[1] implies to me that the concept of True Will is not necessarily incompatible with Christian magick.

> You Angels of Light, I, [Your Magical Name], by the power of the True, Almighty, and Living God, I hereby bid you to depart and accomplish your appointed tasks, in the service of my True Will and to the Glory and Honour of our aforementioned True God to whom you owe loyalty and obedience. I, [Your Magical Name], hereby free the forces constrained, focused, and directed during this operation, that they may go forth and work their various powers upon the manifest universe, for thus is all True Magick and Perfect Power born. By the power of my True Will here embodied by the Magical Name [Your Magical Name], AMEN.
>
> So mote it be.

In our group workings the individual who performed the conjuration gives the License to Depart up to AMEN, and the rest of the group responds with "So mote it be." A solitary magician may wish to include or drop this final statement as desired. When working on my own I generally include it.

If you are working without the ceremonial forms you are essentially done at this point. Finish by knocking once on the Holy Table and stating "I now declare this temple duly closed." When working with the ceremonial forms you will want to close the temple ceremonially before making this declaration. As the AOIVEAE and MADRIAX rituals are designed to encapsulate the evocation itself they should simply be concluded as shown in Chapter 7 prior to the declaration. If you are working with the Golden Dawn ritual forms the manner in which you conclude the operation depends upon its objective.

Today the various Golden Dawn orders generally teach that rituals should be concluded using both the Lesser Banishing Ritual of the Pentagram and the Lesser Banishing Ritual of the Hexagram. As I mentioned in Chapter 7, this is incorrect for most magical objectives

---

1. Augustine of Hippo, In Epistolam Loannis ad Parthos.

because it completely shuts down the ritual as soon as you close the temple. Giving a practical charge more time to operate than the thirty to sixty minutes that are dedicated to a typical ceremonial working will dramatically increase your chances of success. This is accomplished by omitting the Lesser Banishing Ritual of the Hexagram from the closing of your ritual altogether.

For rituals with a target other than yourself you should close with the Lesser Banishing Ritual of the Pentagram. As the pentagram symbolizes the microcosm, this ritual will serve to clear your consciousness of the macrocosmic elements invoked during the rite but allow those elements to continue to operate after you close the temple. It cuts the link between your mind and the spell and, much as stated in the License to Depart, sends the macrocosmic forces back to their proper place so that they can get to work on accomplishing your objective.

For rituals targeting yourself or both yourself and an external target you should close with just the Qabalistic Cross. This serves to balance and ground your consciousness without dismissing the microcosmic elements that you invoked during the rite. Many spells are of this type — for example, if you cast a spell to get a better job you want opportunities to come your way but you also want the magick to affect your body language and attitude so that you seem particularly impressive when a potential employer sets up an interview.

If you are using the Thelemic Star Ruby and Star Sapphire to replace the Lesser Rituals of the Pentagram and Hexagram the same rules apply. Close with just the Star Ruby for a ritual with an external target or the Star Ruby's form of the Qabalistic Cross if the spell targets yourself or both yourself and an external target. I normally use the closing form of this Qabalistic Cross, ending rather than starting with "APO PANTOS KAKODAIMONOS," but I leave that to your discretion based on how you generally perform the ritual.

After performing the closing ceremonial forms, knock once on the Holy Table and declare the temple closed. Your ritual is now complete. At this point, you will want to keep the ritual out of mind while the angels work to accomplish your objective. Some authors contend that in order for a spell to work you must forget the objective completely, but this is difficult in practice and constitutes serious overkill. You can freely remember your working so long as you avoid obsessing or worrying about its outcome. Worry and obsession will undermine a spell just about every time, but simply thinking about it on occasion is harmless.

Chapter 14
Conclusion

ompared to the regions of the Great Table or Watchtowers, and Aires or Aethyrs, the realms inhabited by the angels of the "Heptarchia Mystica" remain relatively unexplored. The latter portions of the Enochian material have been extensively explored by modern magicians for more than a century, while the heptarchial angels have been treated by many as an interesting historical footnote without much practical magical application. As my magical working group found in the course of our exploration of the heptarchial realms this perspective is quite mistaken.

As a simple example, consider the footnote attached to the conjuration for Prince Befafes. If John Dee did indeed summon this Prince to defeat the Spanish Armada in 1588, this would be one of the few cases in history in which a magical grimoire played an important role in a well-documented major world event. For all the attention paid to grimoires such as the "Lemegeton" and the "Key of Solomon", proponents of neither can substantiate similar claims during the entire medieval period or Renaissance. Perhaps another grimoire could have accomplished this feat, but the surviving text seems to imply that if Dee did take such an action it was the angels of the heptarchy to whom he turned.

Grimoire magicians should take note of this, whether they work along strictly traditional lines or incorporate modern ritual forms and structures. My magical working group found that when conjured properly the angels of the heptarchy are both agreeable to magicians and capable of accomplishing much in terms of practical results. Still, even this discovery barely scratches the surface of their true potential, and I invite anyone who has an interest in working grimoire magick to join in and correspond with us regarding their own work with the Kings and Princes.

Secrecy and suppression have set magick back centuries compared to the physical sciences on which our technology is based. In order to bring the art and science of the Magi back into the light of experimental inquiry we must pool our resources and work to develop a standard body of knowledge that is subject to empirical verification and peer review. Since magick involves the workings of consciousness, this is more difficult than it is with hard sciences such as physics, but the science of psychology has confronted the same difficulties and developed many effective methodologies for working with hard-to-define aspects of our experience, such as states of mind.

It is my sincere hope that we as magicians will be able to accomplish the same. Further ritual exploration of the mystical heptarchy may bring us closer to that goal and at the same time provide us with better tools to shape our lives into what we imagine they could be. Study has its place, but in the end there is no substitute for getting on with the work.

Scott Michael Stenwick
Minneapolis, MN

Appendix:
Comselh Ananael
Heptarchial Evocation Ritual

Comselh Ananael is the name that my magical working group chose when we began doing group ritual work in 2002. Since that time we have explored both the Tree of Life and the Enochian universe, and worked extensively with elemental, planetary, and zodiacal forces. Our work with the Heptarchial Kings and Princes was performed using the following ritual, derived from the template found in chapter 6. The ritual has been optimized numerous times over the years and we have found this version to be quite effective for both individual and group operations.

As we work the system from the Thelemic perspective, the ritual structure reflects that rather than the Christian perspective of John Dee and Edward Kelley. Still, much of the methodology is true to the original spirit of the work even when it incorporates modern ceremonial forms.

0. The Temple

The ritual space is set up as explained in Chapter 5. A scrying stone or mirror is placed on the altar cloth above the center of the Sigillum Dei Aemeth. If possible the four smaller Seals should be placed under each of the altar table's four legs. The closer the Temple can be to the Enochian ideal, the better the system will work.

There are two officers in this ritual, Magus and the Scryer. Magus acts as the Officiant and should wear the Enochian ring and lamen. The officers and all others present should wear white robes. The Scryer attempts to contact the conjured spirit or spirits using the mirror or crystal.

The bell chime is placed on western edge of the Table. This should be a chime that can be rung easily with one hand. The Scryer will be ringing it when the Angel or Angels appear, so it must not require much attention to operate. Because of this, its exact position should be left to the Scryer's discretion. A low stool for the Scryer is placed to the west of the altar. It should be of such a height that the stone or mirror is at the Scryer's eye level.

The talisman for the King and Prince of the day is placed on the floor to the west of the altar. It should be reasonable large, since the Magus must stand upon it with both feet when reciting the conjuration. The designs for the talismans are those found in Chapter 11.

I. Opening

All form a circle around the altar. Magus initially stands directly west of the altar and Scryer stands directly east. Magus inhales fully, placing the banishing dagger at his or her lips. The air is then expelled as the dagger is swept backwards.

Magus:
Bahlasti! Ompehda!

Magus then performs the AOIVEAE up to the closing as explained in Chapter 7, moving around the Table and casting in the direction of the Scryer who concentrates on receiving the evoked energies. All present rotate accordingly, so that the entire circle of assembled magicians turns like a wheel as the Magus moves to face each quarter. The idea here is to conjure a line of force that originates with the Magus, passes over or through the stone or mirror, and is received by the Scryer at each of the Temple's four quarters.

Magus:

We take refuge in Nuit, the blue-lidded daughter of sunset, the naked brilliance of the voluptuous night sky, as we issue the call to the awakened nature of all beings, for every man and every woman is a star.

All:

AUMGN.

Magus:

We take refuge in Hadit, the secret flame that burns in every heart of man and in the core of every star, as we issue the call to our own awakened natures, arousing the coiled serpent about to spring.

All:

AUMGN.

Magus:

We take refuge in Heru-Ra-Ha, who wields the wand of double power, the wand of the force of Coph Nia, and whose left hand is empty for he has crushed an universe and naught remains, as we unite our awakened natures with those of all beings everywhere and everywhen, dissolving all obstacles and healing all suffering.

All:

AUMGN.

Magus:

For pure will, unassuaged of purpose, delivered from the lust of result, is every way perfect.

All:

All is pure and present are and has always been so,
for existence is pure joy; all the sorrows are but as
shadows; they pass and done; but there is that which
remains. To this realization we commit ourselves —
pure and total presence. So mote it be.[1]

II. The Magical Field

Magus performs the MADRIAX up to the closing as explained in Chapter 7. As with the AOEVEAE, all present rotate accordingly.

Magus:

MADRIAX CARMARA, YOLCAM LONSHI!

Magus makes the Sign of Rending the Veil, placing hands back to back and then drawing them apart as though opening a heavy curtain.

III. The Preliminary Invocation

All make the Sign of Apophis and Typhon facing the center of the table.

Magus:

Holy art Thou, who art Universe,
Holy art Thou, who art in Nature formed,
Holy art Thou, the Vast and the Mighty,
Source of Darkness, Source of Light.[2]

All make the Sign of Silence, then clasp hands over hearts.

Magus recites the Revised Oration to God as explained in Chapter 7.

Magus:

O Almighty, Eternal, True and Living God: O King
of Glory: O Lord of Hosts: O Thou, who art Heaven

---

1. This section of the opening following the AOEVEAE is adapted from the Refuge and Bodhichitta practices of Vajrayana Buddhism, but has been modified so as to fit with Thelemic cosmology.
2. This revised wording for the Golden Dawn adoration of the Lord of the Universe is adapted from the rituals of the Open Source Order of the Golden Dawn.

and Earth and all things visible and invisible: we beseech Thee in this our present petition to have mercy and compassion upon us, who, faithfully and sincerely of long time have made suit unto Thy Divine Majesty, that we may obtain true Gnosis and full understanding of Thy Divine Wisdom, Power and Goodness. And whereas it has pleased Thee of Thy infinite Goodness, by Thy faithful and holy Spiritual Messengers, to deliver unto us long since an orderly form and manner of Exercise Heptarchial: how, to Thy Honor and Glory, and the comfort of our own souls and of others Thy faithful servants, we may at all times use very many of Thy Holy Angels, their counsels and helps: according to the properties of such their functions and offices, as to them, by Thy Divine Power, Wisdom and Goodness is assigned and limited. Therefore, we heartily and faithfully beseech Thy Divine Majesty to further this our present industry and endeavor to Exercise ourselves, according to the aforesaid orderly form and manner. Grant also unto us this blessing and portion of Thy Heavenly Graces: that thou wilt forthwith enable us, make us apt, and acceptable in body, Soul, and Spirit to enjoy always the Holy and friendly conversation, with the sensible, plain, full and perfect help in word and deed of Thy Mighty, Wise and Good Spiritual Messengers and Ministers generally: and namely of Blessed Michael, Blessed Gabriel, Blessed Raphael and Blessed Uriel: and also, especially of all those which do appertain unto the Heptarchical Mystery and the Mystery of the Great Table. Reveal unto us Thy Majestical Glory, now and forever, through Thy Ministers, the true and faithful Angels of Light.

All:
AMEN. AMEN. AMEN.

Magus rings bell chime.

IV. The Conjuration

The Scryer moves to the west of the altar and is seated at the Holy Table, gazing into the stone or mirror. Magus stands behind the Scryer and all other participants remain in a circle around the Table.

Magus recites the First Key, in Angelic followed by English, and Scryer then recites the Second Key, in Angelic followed by English, as explained in Chapter 9.

Magus performs the Greater Invoking Ritual of the Hexagram for the planet corresponding to the King or Prince, as explained in Chapter 10. Again, all present rotate accordingly except for the Scryer, who remains seated.

Magus then steps onto the talisman and recites the appropriate conjuration for the King or Prince of the Day, depending upon the objective of the rite, as explained in Chapter 11.

Following the conjuration all begin to chant the name or the King or Prince as they visualize the divine light descending into the stone or mirror. When the Scryer sees a vision, he or she rings the bell chime and the chant ends.

V. Charge / Communication

The contents of this section depend on the nature of the ritual as explained in Chapter 12. Either questions should be asked of the summoned King or Prince through the Scryer, as Dee and Kelly did when they received the original system, or the King or Prince should be charged with a particular task. In the latter case, be sure to make note of the exact wording of the Charge.

VI. The License to Depart

Magus gives the License to Depart as explained in Chapter 13. This version of the License is slightly different from the one found in that chapter but will work just as well.

Magus:

O thou [King or Prince's Name], because thou hast-diligently answered unto our demands, and hast been very ready and willing to come at our call, we do here license thee to depart unto thy proper place; without causing harm or danger unto man or beast. Depart, then, I say, and be thou very ready to come at our call, being duly exorcised and conjured by these sacred rites of magick. We charge thee to withdraw peaceably and quietly, and the peace of the Almighty, Eternal, True, and Living God be ever continued between us. AMEN.

All:

So mote it be!

Magus then concludes the MADRIAX as explained in Chapter 7.

Magus:

MADRIAX CARMARA, ADRPAN LONSHI!

Magus makes the Sign of Closing the Veil, bringing both hands together with palms facing as though closing a set of heavy curtains. Scryer then rises and joins the circle, standing opposite Magus.

VII. Closing

All:

May the benefit of this act and all acts be dedicated unto the complete liberation and supreme enlightenment of all beings everywhere, pervading space and time. So mote it be. May the benefits of practice, ours and others', come to fruition ultimately and immediately and we remain in a state of presence. AH![3]

Magus concludes the AOIVEAE as explained in Chapter 7.

Magus:

I now declare this temple duly closed.

One knock with banishing dagger. The rite is at an end.

---

3. As in the Opening, this section is adapted from Vajrayana Buddhism.

Bibliography

Campbell, Colin. The Magic Seal of Dr. John Dee (York Beach, ME: Teitan Press, 2009)

Causaubon, Meric, ed. A True and Faithful Relation of What Passed for Many Years Between Dr. John Dee and Some Spirits (New York, NY: Magickal Childe, 1992)

Crowley, Aleister. 777 and Other Qabalistic Writings (San Francisco, CA: Red Wheel/Weiser, 1986)

Crowley, Aleister. Magick: Book Four (San Francisco, CA: Weiser Books, 1998).

Dee, John. A True and Faithful Relation of What Passed for Many Years Between Dr. John Dee and Some Spirits (Whitefish, MT: Kessinger, 2010)

Dee, John. The Hieroglyphic Monad (York Beach, ME: Red Wheel/Weiser, 2000)

Duquette, Lon Milo. Enochian Vision Magick (San Francisco, CA: Weiser Books, 2008)

DuQuette, Lon Milo. The Magick of Aleister Crowley (San Francisco, CA: Weiser Books, 2003).

DuQuette, Lon Milo. My Life With The Spirits (San Francisco, CA: Red Wheel/Weiser, 1999).

James, Geoffrey. The Enochian Evocation of Doctor John Dee (San Francisco, CA: Weiser Books, 2009)

Kraig, Donald Michael. Modern Magick (St. Paul, MN: Llewellyn, 2010)

Laycock, Donald C. The Complete Enochian Dictionary (San Francisco, CA: Weiser Books, 2001)

Leitch, Aaron. The Angelical Language Volumes I and II (St. Paul, MN: Llewellyn, 2010)

Leitch, Aaron. Secrets of the Magical Grimoires (St. Paul, MN: Llewellyn, 2005)

Lisiewski, Joseph. Ceremonial Magic and the Power of Evocation (Tempe, AZ: New Falcon, 2004).

Peterson, Joseph, ed. John Dee's Five Books of Mystery (San Francisco, CA: Red Wheel/Weiser, 2008)

Peterson, Joseph, ed. The Lesser Key of Solomon (San Francisco, CA: Weiser Books, 2001)

Turner, Robert. Elizabethan Magic (Salisbury, UK: Element, 1990)

Turner, Robert, ed. The Heptarchia Mystica of John Dee (Kent, UK: Aquarian Press, 1986)

Tyson, Donald, ed. Agrippa's Three Books of Occult Philosophy (St. Paul, MN: Llewellyn, 1992)

Tyson, Donald, ed. Agrippa's Fourth Book of Occult Philosophy (St. Paul, MN: Llewellyn, 2009)

Index

D

E

F

G

J

K

L

M

N

O

P

Q

R

S

W

Y

Z

Visceral Magick
Bridging the Gap Between Mundane and Magick

Ever had a "gut feeling" that proved to be correct? Ever gathered up your

courage in the form of "intestinal fortitude"? Modern science has discovered that our digestive organs have a rudimentarty form of consciousness that corresponds to these sayings, and this would be old news to our Celtic ancestors, who believed the human form contained three cauldrons that directed energy, inspiration and wisdom.

This book explores a set of basic experiences, ideas and techniques that used to be at the heart of every magical Tradition, but which are frequently overlooked or ignored in modern times. But they are the very things that breathe life into magical systems, the secret key that makes the magic actually work.

Peter Paddon, author and Witch, has had the fortune to encounter these techniques and practices in several forms, and here he documents his own journey - and the results - as well as laying out exercises and practical applications to enable the reader to stop visualizing and just plain see. Magic is a real force, one that will raise the hairs on the back of your neck, and become a living breathing part of your everyday life. This book will show you how to get there.

$11.95   978-0-9843302-3-2

Other great books available through
www.PendraigPublishing.com
by Raymond Buckland

Buckland's Domino Divination - Fortune-Telling with Dominoes
Although today familiar to most people only as a game, dominoes were originally used by the Chinese for divination and fortune-telling. The reading of dominoes comes under the heading of sortilege and, as such, can be traced back to early Greek and Roman methods of divining the future.

$8.95   978-0-9827263-1-0

Buckland's Practical Color Magick
Color surrounds us in our world and this book can show you how to put that color to work. Color Magick is powerful, yet safe. It is creative and fun to do. It is the use of a natural element in a practical way. Color Magick can be used in meditation, healing, ESP, Tarot, crystal-gazing, ritual, candle-magick, and many other forms of magical practice. Learn all of its secrets in this exciting book!

$9.95   978-0-9827263-9-6

Golden Illuminati
Alec Chambers is in a quandry - his bookstore had been broken into, his storekeeper killed, and everything points to the man behind the mayhem being one of his best customers, Mr. Mathers. But when a very special journal is stolen from his own home, he finds himself in a race across Europe with Mathers and his Golden Dawn compatriots. But how are they to find the answer to the strange cypher code that is their only clue, and what is the identity of the mysterious red-haired woman?

$17.95   978-0-9827263-8-9

CPSIA information can be obtained
at www.ICGtesting.com
Printed in the USA
BVHW082127050819
555133BV00010B/58/P